FIRE KINDLETH FIRE

BLACKIE & SON LIMITED
50 Old Bailey, LONDON
17 Stanhope Street, GLASGOW

BLACKIE & SON (INDIA) LIMITED
Warwick House, Fort Street, BOMBAY

BLACKIE & SON (CANADA) LIMITED
1118 Bay Street, TORONTO

D. M. Jally.

Sudewick

Sudingge Avenue

Blackburn

Feb. 1930

FIRE
KINDLETH FIRE

The Professional Autobiography

of

MARION CLEEVE

Ex-Headmistress of the
Snellham Municipal Secondary School for Girls

Be patient until thou art like unto a well-kindled fire which
turneth into flame and brightness all that is cast into it.
—MARCUS AURELIUS.

BLACKIE & SON LIMITED
LONDON AND GLASGOW
1930

Printed in Great Britain by Blackie & Son, Ltd., Glasgow

AUTHOR'S FOREWORD

The writer of this chronicle had the unusual experience
of spending almost the whole of her professional life—
thirty years—in one and the same school, and of guiding
its development from a very small beginning into a large
girls' school of the kind now called municipal secondary. The increasing importance of this type of education becomes evident as we scan the lists of university
scholarships and honours. The writer hopes that the
story of this development and the portrayal of the intimate
life of such a school may not lack interest to those who
either within the school are doing work of a similar kind,
or without, are furthering the cause of education both
privately in the home and publicly on platform or in
committee room.

The egoism of such a record is inevitable and must
be excused. The book contains no exact portraitures of
either persons or places. As far as the writer knows no
such place as Snellham is to be found, but there are
many resembling it in relevant detail. And, although
the writer knows of no headmistress of the name of

Marion Cleeve, the experiences described herein are real, the opinions and convictions are those genuinely held by a headmistress.

There is romance even within the walls of a classroom. It is apprehended only by those who discern and appreciate potentialities, whose imagination bodies forth the forest while studying the acorn.

CONTENTS

CHAPTER I

Snellham: the Scene of my Life Work

CHAPTER II

Personal Characteristics and Opinions

vii

CHAPTER III

Methods and Principles of Management

CHAPTER IV

Discipline: the Assistant Staff

CHAPTER V

Systems of Discipline

CHAPTER VI

Disciplinary Influences

CONTENTS

CHAPTER VII

The Curriculum: Religious Instruction

CHAPTER VIII

The General Curriculum

CONTENTS

CHAPTER IX

My Experience of the Municipal Control of Education

Fire Kindleth Fire

CHAPTER I

Snellham: the Scene of my Life Work

Snellham, the town in which I spent almost the whole of my professional life, was situated, let us say, in the east Midlands and contained some hundred thousand inhabitants. Its area either formed part of, or was contiguous to, a large coalfield and its destiny was determined by this fact. All coalfields, we are given to understand, are not profitable and cannot be made so; but the Snellham and District coalfield was highly profitable and so were the huge ironworks which had grown up in the neighbourhood.

Le bon Dieu, who so considerately has set large towns beside large rivers, had caused iron and coal to lie in convenient juxtaposition round about Snellham. For whose benefit such happy arrangements are made may be a problem still under discussion in some parts of the world, but, in Snellham, it was solved in favour of the firm of Pigiron Ltd., which owned these collieries and ironworks, and any dissent from this way of thinking was expressed in curses, muttered rather than uttered, when dividends increased and wages decreased. It was, however, generally recognized that the welfare, if not the very existence, of the town was bound up indissolubly with the prosperity of Pigiron Ltd., whose managing directors were resident in or near the town and, directly or indirectly, controlled most of its social and municipal activities. At the beginning of my headship this control was undisputed, but later the influence of Socialism brought changes; there was much defiant talk but little corresponding action. The grip of local capitalism was powerful and Snellham bound fast in misery and iron. The town itself was unattractive, so unattractive as to be a by-word in the surrounding districts. The ridicule it had to bear may have accounted for the otherwise unaccountable devotion of some of those who were called into its service, and I can recall occasions when laughter at its expense ended in such expression as " Poor old Snellham! It's too bad to poke fun at it." Native Snellhamites were very loyal to their town.

The two main thoroughfares, Lombardy Street and Picardy Road, ran parallel for some distance and then converged to a point, or, as a youthful struggler for self-expression phrased it, " they would have been parallel if they had not met in a point farther on ". From that point, five streets branched outwards and upwards and, after a mile or two, led to the so-called residential districts in one of which was situated the Girls' Municipal Secondary School of which I was headmistress for thirty years. On the southern and eastern sides, the town stretched itself out in a relentless succession of slum-like streets lined on both sides with working-class dwell-ings—houses of the meanest, dirtiest type, of which a half-open door would often disclose a filthy interior, broken furniture, paper hanging from walls, pasty-faced babies sprawling and tumbling about. Doors were battered and paintless, windows broken, rags and paper replacing the broken glass, and sometimes the whole fabric—roofing, spouting, masonry—dilapidated beyond repair. Here and there, the sight of clean curtains re-minded one that God's in His heaven, and a polished door knocker set one a-wondering what gallant soul had kept itself alive amid the abomination of general desola-tion. These exceptions, however, were too few and far between to have much effect on the whole, and the scene not only depressed but disgusted. Personally I avoided both sight and sound of such places—a method of ' pass-ing by on the other side ' not uncommon among even those who profess to accept the definition of ' my neigh-bour ' implicit in the parable of the Good Samaritan.

The monotony of the streets was broken by public-houses at every corner and here and there a forlorn little mission church, the former eloquent of the devil and all his works, the latter bearing witness to the truth that Christ came to seek and save the lost. For the rest, Snellham possessed one dirty-looking theatre and its quota of cinemas, music halls, sports grounds, parks, hospitals, churches, and chapels, all well patronized and supported. Football was an important feature in the life of the town, its attendant betting being one great source of excitement. The raucous shouts and cheers of the thousands of spectators at the matches were audible through the murk of wintry Saturday afternoons in every part of the town. For the human mind reaches out and about, seeking a way of escape from dullness and routine, and amusement of some kind is a prime necessity of life to the toilers in mine or factory.

Friends visiting me in Snellham would often ask me where the happy and prosperous people lived, so evident were the signs of depression. Even the shops looked dejected. The draper's finery seemed less fine than in other towns; the grocer's wares more shop-soiled. The fruit at the greengrocer's, usually most alluring to sight and scent, had not the joyous look that ripe fruit often bears on its brightly coloured surfaces—for what shows so cheerful a ' morning face ' as a rosy apple? Blissfully unconscious of any responsibility for the Fall of Man or the Trojan strife, it rejoices openly at being the highly finished product of a great natural process. But in Snellham, even apples were not quite so triumphant, carrots grew flaccid, and lettuces lost whatever heart they had as soon as they were dumped down in Snellham. Only the onion preserved a somewhat dishevelled imperturbability, as if conscious of its unrivalled popularity in Snellham homes. Pawnshops were numerous and flourished exceedingly. I am still trying to forget a description I once heard of an early Monday morning scene when *queues* of women squatted outside one of these establishments, waiting to pawn some of the family clothes to get money for the family breakfast. But the horror I felt has stamped it on my mind. I often *try* to forget—a gloomy sort of business at best and at worst a hopeless one. My subconscious is not so amenable as I could wish and the tendency to depression from which I suffered at Snellham still recurs.

The war brought changes to Snellham. Higher wages and consequent increase in purchasing power gave a fillip to local shop-keeping and, after the armistice, the town presented a much more cheerful appearance. Alas! that the prosperity was short-lived. Writes a friend to me this morning, apropos of the miners' lock-out, " The town is filled with loafing, broken-down men whose clothes hang loosely on their shrunken bodies." In other ways during my sojourn there, there was a gradual improvement in Snellham which was maintained. Some change in the industries of the town cleared the atmosphere of its worst pollution, and the child welfare agencies did a little towards improving matters.

I write these words sitting before an open window through which I have a view of the simple country-side beauty in which my soul delights. I am living among simple, soft-voiced folk in circumstances almost luxurious. At the moment I am conscious of a faint breeze, bringing with it perfume from the flower beds immediately under my windows, and I can hear the chirpings and twitterings of bird life—an eager and pleasing sound. I know, of course, that there is a dark side to country life; that the wages of an agricultural labourer hardly suffice for bare subsistence, and that picturesque cottages are not always happy homes. I realize that the whole creation ' groaneth

and travaileth ', but just now, life is for me exceptionally
serene and there is nothing to remind me of ' old, forgotten, far-off things '.   Yet for some subconscious
reason, my mind darts back to one of my most poignant
experiences.   A. C., a scholarship holder in my school,
whose home was in some such district as I have described,
fell mortally ill with tuberculosis.   I remember her
clearly.   A clever child at the top of the fifth form, frail,
refined, sweet—she had crept unawares into my heart.
When I looked at Alice, I realized what Browning had
in mind when he described the girl-wife in *The Ring
and the Book* as " little Pompilia with the patient brow ".
A patient brow is not at all the same thing as a serene
brow such as Raphael gave to his Madonnas.   The latter
is significant of the ' peace that passeth understanding ',
the former of submission to the inevitable, the difference
lying somewhere about the control of the eyebrows.
The time came when Alice's mother sent for me and I
hastened lest death should forestall me.   The doctor's
motor was at the door and I waited until it had moved
off.   It was a painful waiting.   My soul rose in revolt
as I realized more keenly in what a sordid environment
my gifted little pupil had lived and now lay a-dying.
I felt sick with spiritual conflict as I climbed the rickety
staircase and stood inside the tiny bedroom.   The few
words I spoke to comfort and reassure my young fellow
christian about to ' put out to sea ' sounded hollow and
ineffective.   I longed to beg her forgiveness for having
allowed her to die without knowing ' how good is man's
life, the mere living '.   But, after receiving, as I should

a crown, a kiss wafted feebly by a wasted hand, I turned
and descended into the street. My tears fell helplessly
down the front of my coat as I stumbled home and I
passed a sleepless night, doubting and rebellious. I
was comforted by the recollection of a yellow silk sash
she had worn at our last Christmas party: she had at
least one pretty thing to rejoice over and be proud of.

Every thinking and sensitive person must feel aghast
at the tragedy of unfulfilled lives. How then account
for the slow progress towards improvement? During
my sojourn at Snellham, in spite of the changes due to
the war, there was no decided amelioration in the lot
of the workers. At the hour of the changing of shifts
in the great works, the same undeveloped, stunted men
poured out of the great gates. No one looked cheerful.
The light of pleasurable anticipation was as absent from
their faces as it was when I first stood horror-stricken
at the sight. Perhaps it is that others feel as I did—that
the problem is too difficult to face. I can now recognize
several of the stages through which I passed in my
feeling towards it. First, I refused to think about it at
all. Then, when indifference became impossible, I tried
to wriggle out of the discomfort that thinking brought
to my conscience and susceptibilities. I never got so
far as to quote—as I have heard people quote—Our
Lord's words, " The poor ye have always with you ",
as indicating a state of things that plays a part in the
spiritual education of the race and which will never be
altered. I doped myself with poetical explanations which
in some quite illogical way soothed me for some time.

The thought of thwarted, unfulfilled lives was less painful to my shallow mind when I compared them to:

> Plants in mines that never see the sun,
> But guess at him and strive to reach to him.

The belief is strong in me that struggle is man's path of progress, and the idea of a struggle not ordained of God had not then occurred to me. I read such poems as Miss Underhill's *Uxbridge Road*, which flashes the radiance of a mystic's faith over the dreariness of suburban life, and let my thoughts dwell on the " hidden Spirit's thrust " and on " the race fulfilling the spiral of its steep ascent, predestined of the Will ". But I found no abiding satisfaction and, although I like Blake's poetry as a whole, I came to fret myself when I heard his *Jerusalem* sung. I knew that England is a green and pleasant land only in parts, and that there are comparatively few of us that engage in mental strife and draw the sword in order to build a new Jerusalem, though the *crescendo* may lead us to think we are capable of so doing. Briefly, I did nothing towards solving the problem, but, like many others, while calling myself a Christian, I acquiesced in a state of things directly opposed to Christ's teaching. The most I can say for myself is that I recorded my votes in favour of those who are making the attempt to alter things and refrained from calling them demagogues and self-seekers.

In my dealings with parents I came across many cases of really hopeless poverty which persisted in the struggle to keep a scholarship-holding daughter at school. To see that such heroic people were not disappointed became a passion with me, and had much to do with my organization of the school. I saw to it that scholarship holders were honoured, and that those whose poverty was extreme were not mulcted in regard to the little expenses that school girls incur, keeping the latter as low as possible. I believe that I succeeded in banishing snobbery from the school. In retrospect, I have in this direction little else to claim.

When I first went to Snellham the lack of natural beauty appalled me. I was unaccustomed to life in such surroundings. By far the greater part of my girlhood had been spent within sight and sound of the sea, with intervals of country life, and holidays amid academic surroundings. Ou the long white roads out of Cambridge I learnt to love open spaces, a wide stretch of sky and a blue haze on the far horizon. I have a great love for trees. I delight in the sturdy trees found in the parks of our stately English homes, and in the peculiarly erect grace of the trees of the Lake District. A stunted specimen of what was meant to be so bravely beautiful fills me with a kind of horror, especially if it stretches bare branches from a misshapen trunk, and is outlined against the sky. It suggests such things as workhouses, blasted heaths, and what is aptly described by such adjectives as *misbegotten* and *god-forsaken*. All the trees with which I came into contact in my daily round at Snellham fell short of their full development. Moreover I am constitutionally fastidious. As a child, I cried at the sight of a mangy cat, and loved little pink shells so much

that I insisted on taking them to bed with me, explaining
to a dissenting and sceptical grown-up that I could
" feel the pinkness through the pillow ". The deprivation
at Snellham was a real one, for although the irresistible
urge of springtime brought foliage to our stunted trees
and grass and flowers to our parks and open places—for
Dame Nature is determined in all her ways, watches
closely for opportunities, and is faithful in that which is
least as in that which is much—yet the glory of the green
was soon besmirched and, presently, the only result of
Nature's kindly intention was to make us think what
might have been.

It is natural for human beings to adjust themselves to
what they cannot evade, and I now recognize how certain
habits which I formed unconsciously were the outcome
of Nature's great trick of adaptation. When I was walking
along the streets or waiting at corners for a bus, I was
always watching for a glimpse of what I considered beauty
—a tall chimney stack outlined against a sunset sky; the
white swoop of pigeons through the murky air; the
joie de vivre of a picturesque urchin stealing a ride on the
step of the bus, or of a tiny toddler escaping from his
nurse and laughing back at her from his perilous isolation
at the cross-roads; the swift smooth walk of a simply-
dressed woman or the long balanced stride of a well-
poised man. My friends mistook this preoccupation for
absent-mindedness or indifference to environment. As
a matter of fact, I was defending myself against what
hurt me on the æsthetic side in the same way as I used
poetry to shield me from realism of another kind. The

absence of a clear sky tried me most of all and of this I
was acutely aware at night. When, before getting into
bed, I drew up my blinds and saw no stars, but only a
filthy haze obscuring the heavens, I lay down with something absurdly like that tension of the throat which precedes the visible expression of emotion. A starless sky
seemed symbolic of a God-less world and misty strug-
gling moonbeams of the retarded progress of God's
gracious purposes.

Again without conscious effort, I found a way of escape,
this time by way of auto-suggestion. I do not think I had
ever heard of such a thing, but I practised it regularly
with effect. As I nestled under the bedclothes, I used to
choose something pleasant to think about and allow my
imagination to play round it freely. *Wet violets* were most
often my nocturnal solace. I sometimes woke in the early
morning aware of the dear scent of them on my pillow,
and felt their cool dampness. This predilection I cannot
connect with any outstanding experience in my life, but
so it was. Indeed, although the results stand out clearly
in my memory, I was at the time a little vague as to
what was happening. Another I am better able to trace
was the sounds of cows tugging and tearing at grass and
breathing heavily as they did so. As a child, I once stayed
at a farmhouse, and cows grazed at night under my wide-
opened bedroom windows. In my dreams, the sounds
brought whiffs of fresh, sweet air, very welcome when
Snellham fogs kept all windows shut.

Even after I had fallen asleep, my troubles were not
over. The cessation of ordinary street noises made audible

the clash of railway wagons, the laboured puff-puff of
engines, and the rolling of dust carts; then came the
wail of hooters and the tramp of clog-shod feet. Many
a morning, while dawn was still behind the smoke barrier,
I was wakened by the loud knocking of the professional
knocker-up, or by some poor old workman stopping to
cough and take breath before proceeding to his work.
Mr. Chesterton describes Liverpool workers as going to
work ' when the hooter hoots with their hearts in their
boots '. Such a description is true of Snellham. Hard
joyless work is bad enough, but the heaviest burden a
working-man has to bear is the ever-present fear of what
is popularly known as ' the sack '. Few of those Snellhamites who clogged along in the early morning were
secure of a job, and it was true that their hearts were in
their heavy footwear, lower if possible. Early morning
insomnia stared me in the face. I used to wake with a
startled realization that poverty and suffering were at my
very door. Again I fell back on the defensive, this time
consciously. In imagination I used to revisit the scenes
of some of my most delightful holidays, and usually fell
asleep during the process. I know of no more effective
remedy for insomnia, delightful also in its effect on one's
waking moments. The recesses of Cumbrian Eskdale
figured often in my drowsing mind—especially a little
pinewood, the trees of which stand graciously apart to
allow flickers of sunshine to fall on the loose soil of the
hillock, round which the river runs with a sound as clear
and soft as the water itself; a glimpse, farther up the Dale,
of the sea as it becomes visible in climbing the lower

slopes of Hard Knott Pass; the purpling of the moors at Goathland; the sense of belonging to sea rather than to *terra firma* after a long day spent on Old Lizard Head; and so successfully did I escape from disagreeable matutinal sounds and thoughts that, one morning, while sleepily accepting a cup of tea from my housekeeper, I made a remark which, had it been intelligible, would have been found to refer to the Kyles of Bute.

I was never quite sure whether the less fortunate of my girls were conscious of the sordidness of their environment and envious of those in happier surroundings. Custom does much, adaptation still more, and ignorance may be bliss. Moles are happiest when burrowing, and winged beetles droningly uneasy above ground. Thus may it have been with young Snellhamites. I used to wonder whether it would not make for progress if I drew their attention to it. I know there is such a thing as a divine discontent. Is there also a facile contentment which is of the devil? However that may be, I did nothing to disturb their local patriotism beyond opening their minds to the delights of travel. To destroy is easy; to create, only possible when the Spirit of God moves upon the face of the waters.

When I had been at work in Snellham for a few years, various friends took it upon themselves to warn me against staying longer in ' such a place '. One of these, a dignitary in one of the neighbouring universities, said that Snellham would only throw me on their slag heaps when they had finished with me. I felt the force of his figure of speech as only one who lived among slag heaps and heard the plaints of the aged workless could feel it. I did not explain that I had come to love Snellham, fearing that, although he was one of those who acknowledge the weight of the Imponderables in life, he might not quite understand. It is a mistake to think that only what is lovely evokes love. Why does your little daughter prefer her old rag doll to the lifelike and accomplished beauty which was your last birthday tribute to her? Is it familiarity, old sake's sake? Or, is there something within our human nature which we hardly dare hope for, which eludes the psycho-analyst—something which underlies the question, " Doth He not leave the ninety and nine in the wilderness and go after that which was lost?"— something spiritual, blowing where it listeth, which loves and lavishes divinely where loving and lavishing are most needed?

Snellham was not a happy town, but some virtues flourish in adversity. It was so in Snellham. That section of the townspeople with which I came into official contact was free from certain vices and failings which I detest, notably from that pretentiousness which is the essence of vulgarity. In time we found a point of contact. I came to have a deep regard for them and they came to trust me. If, as she predicted, Queen Mary came to have the name of a town engraved on her heart, I feel sure that a similar surgical operation would disclose a like phenomenon on the heart of Marion Cleeve, and that the name would be Snellham.

CHAPTER II

Personal Characteristics and Opinions

When I have been visiting girls' schools, I have been surprised to see how distinctly traceable, even in such superficial matters as dress, manners, deportment, is the influence of the headmistress. I remember a London school of which the headmistress was of the old-world type. While I was there, I felt in an atmosphere of ringlets, lavender, and Milton's sonnets. Headmistress, staff, girls, all conveyed the impression of old-time dignity and sweetness. Another school produced the impression of lumpishness and heavy mirth—rather like the dumpling served at school dinner, solid, toothsome, and excellently cooked. During that meal the headmistress made a pun involving two languages, which had to be explained before we could pay our tribute of appreciative laughter. That certain schools tend to produce certain types is easily explicable; but that characteristics, not in themselves quite admirable, should be imitated is a fact which deserves more attention than we give it. It would seem that our children are helpless before us; willy-nilly, consciously or unconsciously, they receive our impress, and the educator, parent or teacher, rules the world.

The wisdom of Providence in hiding the future from us is justified of her children. The uncertainty of what is round the corner lends zest to existence, inspires effort and leaves room for hope. Also, it allows the mind to busy itself with conjectures as to what might have been the effect if something had happened which did not happen, or if something had not happened which did happen. I indulge in conjecturings of this kind. I was not appointed head of the Snellham Municipal School for Girls as the result of personal application. I was pushed towards, and pitch-forked into, that position by what seemed like Fate, and the experience was so topsy-turvying in its effect that I was too much dazed— after describing a mental and moral parabola of experience—and too utterly preoccupied with recovering my perpendicular, to do anything but accept the charge. I am still debating whether if I had had time to reflect I should have chosen as I did. I have never regretted my choice. I found in Snellham a sphere of happy work which is one of the choicest gifts of the gods.

If the appointment of the Snellham headmistress had been left to me, I should not have appointed myself. I should probably have interviewed myself and then turned down the application after endorsing it as ' lacking in personality '. It would have been a mistake, for I have never lacked personality, but always what is curiously termed *presence*, which is by no means the same thing. In *Vice Versa*, a book which used to make us laugh two or three decades ago, the unfortunate Mr. Bultitude, when first encountering his schoolboy tormentors as one of themselves, was met by the question, " Would you rather be a greater fool than you look or look a greater fool than you are?" At any stage of my career, had I been taxed in the same way, I should have replied, " I would rather be a greater fool than I look." My limitations were ever before me. Even my physique, never very robust, seemed less capable than it was, and that there was something amiss with my manner may be deduced from the fact that I was half-way through my headmistress-ship before strangers ceased to conclude that I was my secretary, and were suspiciously profuse in their apologies when their mistake was brought home to them.

A great English essayist, whose insight is as clear as his style of expressing his opinions, says that if a person's appearance is against him, there is sure to be something lacking in his character, and that the first impression a man gives you, answers most nearly to the idea he has of himself. Both these dicta were true in my case. I was unimpressive in appearance, not wholly unattractive, but certainly undistinguished, and I lacked that amount of self-conceit which is needed for self-confidence and which I came to recognize later as part of the normal development of youth.

The same writer goes on to say that modesty is the least of the virtues, and is a confession of the deficiency it indicates. I am not sure that Hazlitt is right about the deficiency: modesty may be caused by the over-valuation of the qualities of others, not by depreciation of one's own. I believe it was so in my case. I began life with a tendency to accept people at their face value, and disillusionment was one of the sadnesses of my life.

One effect of my lack of presence was that people were inclined to give me advice, to which I listened meekly without, however, always acting upon it. With a surprising unanimity, visiting inspectors and examiners exhorted me not to work so hard. " It is not the part of a head to *do* but to *be* and to make others do," was the comfortable advice of one such official who, I came to believe, practised some part of what he preached. My experience taught me that a head has both to do and to be, and that the former depends upon the latter.

On the evening of my—somewhat unexpected—appointment a friend whose opinions I had reason to respect gave me some of the most useful advice I ever had. " You will have," he said, " to face many difficult situations, and encounter much that is hard to bear. That is inevitable in public life. Remember that, speaking generally, men appreciate right doing. You may meet with exceptions but the generality of men admire righteousness even when they do not practise it." My friend's faith in his fellowmen was justified as a whole. I believe most men admire righteousness and that some few practise it. The argument that a certain course must not be taken because it is not just, or kind, or straightforward, does not carry all before it as it should. Even those who profess to live by strict codes were, in my experience, not to be trusted when it came to personal considerations and, in practice, were as unreliable as the so-called man of the world, who is reputed to stick at nothing. The exigency of the moment is the test. "Don't you trust me, Miss Cleeve?" asked one. "I trust no one but myself," I replied. It was the summing up of much experience, and only slightly an overstatement. Disillusionment is hard to bear and "lilies that fester smell far worse than weeds". One result of my friend's emphasis on righteousness was that the word stuck to me, and I came to admire the virtue it connotes as strong and practical—one which allows of no hedging and is free from sentimentality. This ideal I passed on to my girls. (Is it possible for a head to have any sort of ideal and not pass it on to her school?) For more than twenty-five years, I never opened school without reading the Collect for Daily Grace, and, as I prayed "that all our doings may be ordered by Thy governance, to do always that is righteous in Thy sight", I felt I was asking the best and safest for the young people whose bowed heads were before me.

The same friend went further with his kindly advice. "If ever you are hesitating," he said, "between two courses of action, the one being more merciful than just, the other more just than merciful, decide on the former. Your mistake, if you make one, will then be on the right side." This counsel served me in good stead hundreds of times, and, if ever he and I meet in the spirit world and still retain the memories of past doubts and fears, I shall thank him for enabling me to profit by his keen insight and fine spiritual valuations. A fixed principle of action makes the life of an administrator much easier. The fact that there are nearly always two sides to a question leads often to painful hesitancy and indecision. No one principle meets every case, but this was applicable to many. A headmistress's responsibility in deciding as to the necessity for, and the nature of, punishment, in estimating character and passing judgment on work and so forth, is a very heavy part of her burden.

The presiding examiner at my first Local Examination centre—who, incidentally, was a cousin of Lord Kitchener —advised me as follows: " Never have rows. Rows will hurt you more than they hurt the other fellow. Clever people get their own way without rows. If you can't get it, go without it, but in any case *don't have rows.*" I got my own way and had no rows for twenty-five years. My instrument of school government was definite in assigning ' sole control ' to the headmistress on all important points and, for the rest, I went without what I couldn't get. A friendly town clerk, who found a few months at Snellham as much as he could stand, and who was kind enough to warn me to ' get out of it as soon as you can ', made an effort to put me wise about the peculiarities of committees. " Committees," he said, " don't vote from conviction as you would do. Half of the members don't know what they are voting about. There are always one or two who count. Your easiest course is to get hold of the one or two." There was some strain in me that kept me from doing this. I rarely sought interviews with the mighty, preferring to get along on my own. I never had a chairman who was both intelligent and leisured; when they weren't too stupid to be of use, they were too busy to be of service. So I formed the habit of transacting all external business through the director of education, and devoted my time to the special work of the headmistress within the school building, a monthly meeting, sometimes almost a formality, being my only point of contact with my governing body. This I now admit was unwise. I cannot say that I regret a course of action which made my career so free from interference and allowed me more time for essentials. If I were to use a current and hideous expression, I should say that I ' cut the cackle ' and got to the business. This town clerk, who had few illusions about municipal government, went on to say: " If the committee refuse anything you are really keen about, let the matter drop at once. Provided no resolution has got on the minutes, they will forget all about it and, by and by, when you bring it up again you may get it." That happened many times. I left Snellham without a vestige of respect for the intelligence of committees.

My lack of presence had a more unpleasant consequence in that it exposed me to the attentions of any bully who crossed my path. Bullies were numerous in Snellham: industrialism breeds them. The ' verray parfit, gentil knight ' type of man did not abound there, though, as I have good reason to remember, it was represented. My memory lingers happily over two fine specimens of that fine genus: the one was, it seemed, instinctively chivalrous; the other not only so, but also a close follower of the Captain of all chivalrous souls. Both sprang to arms quickly when occasion required.

I am afraid that I ran away from bullies. That was unwise. Man is not meant to be craven—to run away. If he does, he suffers. If he fears, he falls a prey, whether to disease, or a barking dog (which means no harm, but cannot resist a flying pair of heels), or a bully whose worst instincts are roused when he sees his victim flinch. I am told that even an infuriated bull will change his mind if he senses courage—but I shall never put one to the test. But even the devil turns tail if we resist him, and I am sure that courage is its own reward.

The chief weapon of the bully is the lie. A municipal secondary school headmistress is the most defenceless of public officials. She must stand foursquare whatever missiles are hurled at her. She may not state her case publicly because she has the dignity of her school to uphold, and, in the wordy warfare, injury may be done to that which is dearer to her than personal advantage. This motive for preferring obloquy to self-vindication is not of the kind to be appreciated by the bully and his seconders, who will mistake it for weakness and be encouraged thereby. There are degrees in lying; the cruelest of all is the lie which is the bearing of false witness.

Last night I had just written these words about false witness when a nightingale in the garden below suddenly burst into song. I put out my light and listened. The rapture continued for some moments, and then stopped dead. Straining my eyes in the darkness I saw the hovering form of a hawk a few feet above the lawn. The revulsion of feeling was painful: the beauty of the song had replaced the dark thoughts which were crowding into my mind about the cruelty of the bearing of false witness and was, in its turn, driven out by the sight of the hawk's tense poise. I remembered that the poet who sang of the beauty of the nightingale's song, sang also of a world ' where men sit and hear each other groan '. I became aware of that ' still sad music of humanity ' which the Hebrew writers call, more aptly, it seems to me, and much more forcibly, a *cry*. The word *cry* obsessed me. I called to mind some of the passages in the Bible in which it occurs: " And the Lord said, because the *cry* of Sodom and Gomorrah is great I will go down and see whether they have done according to the *cry* of it "; " The soul of the wounded *crieth* out ". I remembered how Isaiah connects righteousness with a *cry*: " He looked for judgment and behold oppression, for righteousness and behold—a *cry*." The wail of those who have been done to death by the bearing of false witness—we call it slander—is prolonged to our day when some of the grosser forms of cruelty have ceased. It was the weapon used against our Lord, and the thought that, by patient endurance of the ordeal by slander, we may gain that fellowship with His sufferings which the saints have longed for and sought after, is the greatest solace I can suggest to my colleagues in distress.

Our increased appreciation of the force of suggestion should make us regard slander with increased horror. The assassin stabs in the dark; the murderer weaves his deadly webs in secret. Both destroy what has a right to continued existence. Slander may be likened to them. In secret it often originates; its aim is the destruction of something more precious than life, whether it be the reputation of a life-time built up with care and self-sacrifice, or what we mean by the word *honour*. The Mosaic code, with fine appreciation, recognized in the bearing of false witness, a crime to be classed with murder and theft, and rightly so, for slander both robs and kills. " Take honour from me and my life is done," says Norfolk in *Richard the Second*, and we express the same fact in our proverb, " Give a dog a bad name and hang him." But before the disclosures of modern psychology we may not have recognized that even the well-disposed man is helpless before the oft-repeated lie, unless he definitely rouse himself to repudiate it. Once accepted, it will probably reappear later in some such vague statement as, " I have heard something to that effect before." The God-fearer needs to be on his guard against ' taking up a reproach against his neighbour ' and the Christ-lover— the follower of Him who said, " Neither do I condemn thee "—when called upon to exercise his critical faculty, needs to divest his mind of prejudice. There is no doubt that lying and slandering are on the increase. They are by way of becoming a political device and even the dead are not sacrosanct.

I am of opinion that the virtue of tolerance is overdone, and that such evils as bullying and slandering flourish because of a travesty of so-called christian charity which condones where it should condemn. It is hard to be angry and sin not, and the fear of injuring our own chances of salvation may lead to a neglect of the duty of christian anger. Moreover, the readiness to forgive other people's enemies is often suspiciously like the easy condonation of wrong which does not affect our personal interests. We are not told to forgive everybody's enemies and I for one do not intend to do so. There is such a thing as spiritual indolence which makes us so undiscriminating that the children of darkness in their generation appear wiser than the children of light.

No christian can fail to recognize the emphasis Our Lord placed on the forgiveness of those who trespass against us. It is one of the most thought-provoking characteristics of the christian religion that it makes a dead set at our natural instincts. I believe that true forgiveness is impossible to unaided man. Meekness is even now an unpopular virtue. A headmistress of my acquaintance was the subject of slanderous attack originated by one of her women governors. Years passed and both slanderer and slandered grew old in an atmosphere of lies and intrigue. At length, the former fell ill, made a death-bed repentance, sent for the woman she had wronged, and in the presence of the clergyman said in effect, " I know I have made your life a hell on earth, but I am dying. Will you forgive me?" My friend replied, " I can't." I was disappointed that she did not recognize that from a christian standpoint repentance should evoke forgiveness even to seventy times seven. But I refrained from judging my friend, knowing that the springs of her life had been poisoned and her usefulness impaired. " I spoke only the truth," she explained

on the only occasion on which she was heard to refer
to the incident, the memory of which is a nightmare to
me. It had the effect of making me read into the prayer
that we may be delivered from " Envy, hatred, malice,
and all uncharitableness ", a petition that I might be
saved from ever inspiring in anyone's heart such a hatred
that even the approach of death is powerless against it.
It sometimes happens in the life of the soul that we come
to an *impasse*; our spiritual progress is stopped by a
jungle growth so dense and so mephitic that only the
grace of God avails to save us from death. Of all such
poisonous growths one of the most deadly is the stifled
hatred which results from slanderous attack.

I have just finished reading a novel in which the description of a freakish headmistress caught my attention,
because it included the statement that ' real people could
not bear to be near her '. Are there any *real* people?
I am not deceived by the current craze for a simplicity
which is complicated; unaffectedness is the current
affectation and unconventionality is by way of becoming
conventional. Possibly the writer meant that the headmistress was so much of a sham that people who were
shams in a less degree steered clear of her. That would
happen as a matter of common experience. Although I
lack sincerity, I exact a certain amount of that basal
virtue from my friends, preferring, for that very reason,
much friendship to many friends. I often recognize my
friends' sincerity from gaps in their conversation, which
I attribute to their reluctance to disagree with me coupled
with a determination not to pretend to do otherwise.

These conversational *lacunæ* make me long to shake them, while increasing my love and respect for them.

When it comes to sincerity we all live in glass houses, though the thickness of the glass may vary a little. In Snellham, we usually had on hand a public character who had managed so to impress his fellows, that they called him ' honest Jim ' (or Joe, or Tom, or Dick). (Why does this conspicuous sort of ' honesty ' lodge so often in the breasts of men whose christian names admit so easily of monosyllabization? We were never afflicted with ' honest ' Archibalds or Marmadukes.) Closer acquaintance with these notables forced me to the conclusion that the so-called honesty was only outspokenness and insensitiveness to people's feelings. The downright man is seldom a gentleman in the best sense of the word, and often the reverse of upright. Once when our local ' honest ' Bob (or Sam or Bill) was heard to refer to his own honesty, a friend opined that he might be an honest humbug. The epithet hit the mark: that is what many of us are—*honest humbugs*.

Self-examination is a painful process, and self-knowledge—if there is such a thing—must be terrifying in the extreme. Many of the great saints seem to have been scared into holiness by a sight of themselves as they really were. I doubt whether even Aristotle himself realized the whole implication of his injunction *Know thyself*, for the Greeks seem untroubled by the hideousness within. Not so the contemporary Hebrew—witness the fifty-first psalm, in which we see a human soul in an agony of self-abasement. How he beats it out! " Have mercy upon me; according to Thy mercy blot out my transgression; I was born in sin; create in me a clean heart; wash me throughly from my sin; renew a right spirit within me." Seekers after God in all ages seem to have been either goaded towards Him by a sense of unbearable pollution, or drawn upward by the beauty of His Holiness. The Jew travelled by the path of penitence. Did the Greek seekers find Him in their quest for truth and beauty?

My experience leads me to believe that young souls travel upward by what is perhaps the less travelled track—the quest for truth and beauty. The idealism of youth is, I think, one of the most cogent reasons for belief in the existence of such a God as ours. Otherwise, whence comes it? Before I realized that there was a God who answers prayer, I guessed there was one. I was convinced that there was something, some power, in the world which could not be apprehended by the senses. I discerned it in the wisdom of great poets, in the altruism of some of my fellows, and in what I have called the idealism of youth. I watched the effect on young minds of association with beautiful things and concluded that it was not of the earth, earthy. It became clear that there was something uplifting in the influence of great master-pieces of literature and art. Also, I came to know what Ruskin meant when he said that ' the sweetness of the common dawn was to him a call to self-dedication '. When I passed on to the consideration of moral beauty I found the Cross at the centre—the eternal symbol of beauty born out of what is hideous—God's ideal for both race and individual, the brutish to become the divine. In a flash I saw that the words, " He that loveth his life shall lose it " were not a meaningless paradox, but the expression of an eternal truth; that ' the spiral of man's steep ascent ' was by means of sacrifice; that the sacrificial life, being in harmony with the divine purpose, brought peace and power; that the beauty which touches men's hearts and makes them worship has in it the element of sacrifice, and that striving and sacrifice are essential elements in the spiritual evolution of the race.

The pivot on which all personal religion turns is the possibility of communion between the human soul and God. It is impossible to prove that there is a God; it is also impossible to prove that there is not a God. The matter is settled for ever when spirit meets Spirit. Efforts to describe this communion must always fail in as much as the language of the material universe is insufficient when it comes to the expression of the spiritual. In the Bible such efforts have resulted in legend, apocalypse, poetry, and prose which becomes poetry when the throb of the Spirit becomes too intense for prose. Much of the interest of the Bible records is here. What really happened to the man called Jacob when he is represented as waking from sleep and saying, " Surely the Lord is in this place?" Elijah must have passed through strange experiences to be expressed only in terms of Nature's dreadest manifestations before he stood at the door of the cave and received his message in what the literal Hebrew describes as ' *a sound of thin silence* '. In the play, *St. Joan*, when Robert suggests that her voices are due to imagination, Joan replies, " O yes, that is how God sends His messages to us." I recall the exact sound of Miss Thorndike's voice as she uttered those words. There was a happy finality about it as though, for the speaker, the matter was settled happily and for ever, and a thrill that was almost a throb. The sound reminded me of a thrush's song on a spring morning, when rapture presses out rapture and melody crowds on melody until the little throat seems like to burst. I can believe that hundreds of Miss Thorndike's hearers endorsed those words, the perfect expression of which may have been due to a joyous conviction of their truth, or merely to the perfection of her art.

At Snellham it was impossible to avoid thinking about the nature of the work on which so many of the towns-people were engaged, and ' thinking sometimes makes the heart so sore '. My heart used to ache for the intelligent working man engaged, year in, year out, on work in which it was impossible to take an intelligent interest. What a mind-deadening drudgery, to be replaced when strength failed by a poverty-stricken old age! I have heard a teacher's life described as drudgery because, forsooth, it involves line upon line and precept upon precept. Those who speak thus do not know the meaning · of the word as we knew it in Snellham, and are far from realizing the glorious opportunities of a teacher's life. In one respect it is unsurpassed—from beginning to end it may be made sacrificial.

Envy is often misplaced. A friend of mine was once expostulating with someone for lavishing expensive gifts

upon her. " Don't stop me," was the unexpected reply,
" I have to watch for opportunities for self-denial, and
it is so hard for me to be generous." Since I first saw
G. F. Watts's picture *For he had great possessions*, and
noted the droop of the head and shoulders and the mani-
fest depression of the whole figure of the rich young
ruler as he turns away from Christ, I have allowed my
imagination to play round the scene. Did he, I wonder,
soon mingle with a crowd and thus be lost to sight? Or
did Jesus—Who, beholding him, loved him—and the
Twelve watch him as he made his way along the dusty
road, each leaden footstep increasing the distance between
himself and the Master Who, being even then on His
way to the Cross, knew so well the secret of happy and
successful living? Was the heart of Jesus saddened, and
was there a long pause before He turned to His disciples
and said, " How hardly shall they that trust in riches
enter the Kingdom!"?

Mr. Chesterton says that our principle of life is the
most important thing about us, and that a landlady is
less likely to lose her rent if her lodger is poor and honest
than if he is rich and conscience-less. It may well be that
everyone lives, consciously or unconsciously, by some
code or other. I feel sure that codes are bound to reveal
themselves in some such utterances as the following:
" Though I fear not God, neither regard man "—the
code of the libertine and daredevil; " How can I do this
great wickedness and sin against God "—the code of
the God-fearer; " The love of Christ constraineth me,"
the code of the Christ-lover; " I'm out to have a good

time," a modern and unintelligent version of " Let us eat and drink for to-morrow we die ". Not that we act always in accordance with our code—better sometimes, worse perchance—but the general trend of our life is determined by it.

In describing anyone's code it ought to suffice if we say ' he is a christian ', for if that term implies anything, it certainly implies a principle of life. Is the word *christian* losing some of its force and distinction? Two church-workers were discussing the virtues of their respective spiritual pastors and masters. One declared that hers was a ' good christian man '. " He may be," replied the other, " but mine is a *real* christian." The same distinction was made with more detail by my housekeeper when I inquired how her brother, a churchwarden, liked his new vicar. " Oh fine," she replied, " he says we've got a christian now." When I had recovered from shock, I asked the obvious question about the late vicar. " Yes, he was a christian all right, but this one is a *real* christian: he's got more of a soul; the other was all for getting the church on." (I am interested to note that the one of the more developed soul is now a bishop; he of the less developed achieved only a deanery.)

What these simple people vaguely realized is that the name *christian* is applied to any kindly person whose morals pass muster, who attends church or chapel with some degree of regularity and who subscribes to the church funds. Possibly we are right in so applying it. But a *real* christian is something much rarer, much more powerful, much lovelier, and as easily distinguishable as a snowy peak among grassy hillocks. A real christian bears the sign-manual of Christ received, probably, during some indescribable, spiritual experience—such as I have referred to as the subject of prime importance in the Bible records. He lives on a higher plane, for his life is hid with Christ in God. Outsiders discern in him a soul centre—a centre of calm and certainty; a centre of peace and joy; a centre which is also a powerhouse of influence whence issue impulses to help and heal.

A headmistress or headmaster may be highly qualified in every academic and professional respect. but the lasting success of the school will depend on her or his principle of life, which cannot remain long in doubt. It will influence pupils, staff, parents; it will leave its mark on time-tables, syllabuses, curricula, and be traceable in examination records and games arrangements. The tone of the school depends upon it.

Christ-lover, God-fearer, self-lover—grades and shades innumerable—but the greatest of them all is the Christ-lover.

CHAPTER III

Methods and Principles of Management

In retrospect I find much satisfaction in realizing the vastly higher value now placed on children than was the case when I began my official life. " All that is needed for education," said the first chairman of the Snellham education committee, only partly in joke, " is a boy, a man, and a cane." Another member of the same committee, when exasperated by demands for school extension, vented his feelings as follows: " They talk about children being an asset to the nation. Nonsense. I say there are too many children. I wish I could get hold of some of the fathers." (This outburst, I must explain, preceded our use of the word *cannon-fodder*, and was probably due to irritation at the expression *living wage*, which was then just becoming general.) At the first committees I attended, the opinion that what was good enough for the fathers was good enough for the children was accepted as a commonplace. Nowadays, it would be regarded as a sign of municipal ineptitude.

The war had much to do with the change. The most conscience-less ruler, should such a specimen be extant, would not now dare to say, "Après moi le déluge", nor would a modern Hezekiah, after listening to prophecies of national disaster, calmly remark, " Good, if peace and truth be in my days." Civilization acknowledges more definitely than ever before its responsibility for the race. *Le jour est aux enfants*.

I was already a headmistress when the responsibility for the supply of secondary education was taken over by the borough and county councils, and, as my school was soon municipalized, I am able to speak confidently about the development and distinctive character of that new type of school which we call municipal because it is maintained out of the rates and, therefore, managed by governors chosen from the borough council. For these reasons, these schools have the advantage of being the objects of civic pride—a fact which ensures fine buildings and adequate equipment. The children attending them are often the pick of the primary schools—keen, determined to make good, and above the average in intelligence. It is true that they have often to carry burdens of home worries, but for this there may be compensation in the moral sphere. When is a handicap not a handicap?

The obligation to maintain a high standard of work is specially binding on the heads of municipal schools: in no other way is a university career opened to the clever child of the worker. Genius is wayward in its incidence, the wind blowing, apparently, where it listeth, and we cannot afford to bury ' mute inglorious Miltons ' or potential Cromwells. The specialization classes of municipal schools should be well catered for.

The working-class child who shows no special aptitude for advanced work is in no less need of every assistance his school can give him. Never was the struggle for existence, for a foothold on the ladder, so desperately fierce as to-day. Every head of a school who comes into contact with anxious parents and prematurely anxious boys and girls, must feel the urge of effort to secure for each and all a creditable school-leaving certificate. This is not easy. It involves the insistence on a capable set of conscientious teachers, not only in the examination forms but throughout the school, and how difficult this task is, only those who have essayed it can tell. Again, the delight of experimenting in novel systems and educational methods has to be foresworn: a failure might mean damage to the careers of less able pupils of that year, because experimenting generally means the trying of one thing after another—a sure way of losing time. It is a kind of gambling in children's futures, and the temptation to ' show off ' as a pioneer is one of the subtlest in the devil's repertory, because it has all the appearance of a virtue. Indeed the strength and subtlety of it makes me suspect that there is a bit of the pedagogue in the devil. He certainly knows how hard it is for a leader to follow tamely instead of forging ahead in his own fashion.

The girls in my school belonged to all classes except the very rich, but it is the presence of large numbers of working-class children that imparts to municipal schools their distinctive character and, in my opinion, adds to the interest of their administration. Things that move are vastly more interesting than those that don't, and climbing, striving, even pushing are all signs of vitality. To travel, hopefully or otherwise, is better than to have arrived and settled down. There was a fascinating kind of strength about my girls. Somewhat lacking in grace, they were abundantly endowed with grit. My spirit rose to heights it would never have reached, had I not felt that I was captaining young, earnest souls who pressed on me from behind.

The secondary school child who comes from a working-class home needs much of what may be described as *child nurture*, to replace the home training which their parents are often unable to give—owing to wage-earning occupation, lack of domestic help, &c. An atmosphere favourable to culture has to be diffused. Hindrances, such as eccentricities of manner, need loving and careful attention; grudges have to be smoothed away, snags of all kinds straightened out. It must needs be that these offences come, and happy is he who is able to make crooked places straight and rough ones smooth.

In the world of pedagogy, especially on the feminine side of it, there is a tendency to move in a vicious circle, inasmuch as the taught of one generation become the teachers of the next. Hence the persistence of type among headmistresses, and to some extent among head-masters. It is a matter for professional congratulation that the former have not become the butt of the low comedian as have mothers-in-law and spinster aunts. What is steadfast inspires respect; what is stereotyped invites ridicule. At times I myself have felt absurd when acting what I considered the appropriate part of a headmistress: the disparity, between what I knew myself to be and what I was trying to appear, was disconcertingly great. The danger is largely a thing of the past: the war took the starch out of most of us, and the alarming trend of feminine fashions has had the same effect. It is impossible for a present-day headmistress to feel, much less to act, like her predecessors: a shingled head and abbreviated skirts are not compatible with the style and ideals of headmistresses who were hampered by constant responsibility for the correct disposal of wide-spreading and trailing draperies, and whose coiffures owed more to chance than to design. I was a headmistress before this emancipation took place, and when I first took office the hand of tradition lay heavy upon me. It was a long time before I dared to be myself as well as the headmistress of the Snellham Municipal School for Girls. I admired the solid dignity, culture and devotion of the headmistresses I used to meet, say, at the annual meetings of our Association. These qualities are hard to beat. There were giants in those days and they assumed, perhaps too appropriately, the demeanour of giants.

Of my own headmistress—I was educated at a publicly managed boarding-school—I remember only unimportant details—such as a gown she wore made of thick black and old-gold striped silk, which trailed behind her as she made a stately descent down the spacious and thickly-carpeted staircase (out of bounds to us girls) into the main corridor, disappearing from our sight as the door of her sanctum closed behind her; well-starched maids, who ushered therein visitors, often black-coated and clerical in appearance, and, at other times, carried in what we understood to be cups of beef-tea. Not that she was in any way delicate—my impression is to the contrary—but, in those days, rude health was considered rude, and adventitious bowls of beef-tea may have been a social necessity for so refined and important a lady. She read prayers in a very *consecrated* voice which awed us into what we mistook for devotion, and I believe she taught us Scripture, although I actually recall only one lesson—probably it required a map of Joshua's conquests, and I was always ' bad at ' maps. I may add that, out of the thousands of Bible lessons that I must have had in the course of my school education from her or anyone else, this is the only one I remember anything about. Nevertheless the school dominated me; indeed it dominated us all. More or less slowly, but very surely, it—or they—got us. We came to think as they—or it— thought and did as we were told. We passed our days in a little world of our own, and I wept hot tears when I had to leave it.

Some years passed before I made the astounding discovery that I disliked the thought of my old school, and was vaguely resentful of some wrong done to me there. Gradually it became clear to me that what I was happiest about when I thought of my old school was that I didn't cave in at once to the school spirit—I needed some breaking in. The tone, I must explain, was considered excellent and, if I had been suddenly questioned about it, I should have so described it. Discipline was enforced by a system of credit marks, for *conduct*, *punctuality*, and *neatness*, three each *per diem*. If we lived a blameless life for a week we grew richer in respect of each of the three cardinal virtues aforesaid by eighteen marks. If we managed to do so for a term of twelve weeks, we were credited with some two hundred marks in each. We lost a neatness mark for dropping a hanky, a punctuality mark for not having our gloves fastened to time, a conduct mark for not speaking correctly or using our mother tongue when French was prescribed, &c., &c. For really heinous offences, such as giggling, we had a 'bad mark' in conduct, which took away ten at one fell swoop, two of that kind making us bankrupt for that week. To my past dismay and my present satisfaction, my first report was to the effect that I was minus ninety-eight in conduct, nine in punctuality, and had only five left in neatness. Result—a lecture from my father, and many heart-to-heart talks with mistresses and Sixth Form girls—we had no prefects in those days. Being at the sentimental age, I thoroughly enjoyed these talks and would fain have gone on losing marks so that the thrill of them might continue, but the paternal influence was too strong for me to incur the risk. I became a reformed character, and, try as I may, I cannot even now shake off the feeling of being one. Thus are we scarred in our youth by the well-meant efforts of the unwise.

As a headmistress I developed a loathing for private interviews with girls, and more often than not conducted them on the doormat outside my door. They were of the kind best described as crisp, keen and kindly. Sentimentality, which in girls' schools usually degenerates into *schwärmerei*, works havoc with the spirit of jolly comradeship which is characteristic of the best type of school.

My feeling of resentment is not against anyone in particular but against a system. I am ashamed at having yielded to a kind of spiritual tyranny. The feeling persists: I am often within walking distance of the school, which is externally one to be proud of, but I have never entered it since the day I left it in tears.

I believe this kind of spiritual domination was common in those days and even later. It is quite possible that I was heading for something of the sort when an access of common sense came to the rescue. Most girls, I noticed, disliked being thought ' good at school '. I was once so fortunate as to have on my staff two mistresses who were described in the report of a Full Inspection as ' outstanding personalities ' as well as good teachers. They were both dear things of whom I was proud. During one of the annual meetings of our Association, I vented my pride in conversation with the headmistresses of the two high schools at which they were educated. " I have to thank your school for an excellent mathematic specialist," I began, and was proceeding to dilate when I was interrupted. " The most troublesome girl I ever had in the school, grossly insubordinate," &c. Shortly afterwards I addressed much the same words to the headmistress of my able science specialist. The answer came with equal spontaneity. " Isn't she a treasure? Never had a minute's anxiety about her. The best girl on earth." I repeated all this to the two concerned. One was delighted with the bad account of her as a schoolgirl; the other begged me not to mention it again, adding, " I was disgustingly good at school." There was something wrong with the discipline in those days: the girls who were too easily submissive, were dominated. There is less danger in that direction nowadays, but it is just as well for us all to remember that ' it's an awkward thing to play with souls ' and that there is such a thing as reaction in the moral sphere. The almost complete system of self-government which I adopted later was the result of these experiences.

We lose much time in groping for ideals, and at best the span of our working life is very short. If only ideals could be handed on to those who have lived up to them and found them good! But ready-made ideals, I judge, would lack dynamic in the way of what the psychologists call *affect*. One can but suggest. The ideal I worked my way up to was that of free growth. I annexed it from a passage in the second book of Samuel, which runs as follows: " One (R.V.) that ruleth over men must be just, ruling in the fear of God. And he shall be as the light of the morning when the sun riseth, even a morning without clouds; as the tender grass springing out of the earth, by clear shining after rain." These words are descriptive of one of nature's beautiful transformation scenes, and there can be no finer ideal of the effect of influence. I have known characters whose influence was as ' the shadow of a great rock in a weary land ' and rested gratefully under such. But with the young—not rest but growth. Here is a ' growing morning ', as we call one in which we can fancy we hear the sap rising and see the tendril yearning; the rain has cleansed and refreshed; the sunlight fosters and allures upward; the clouds are scattering before the sun and all is health-giving and beautiful. Such an influence leads to free development into beauty and ultimate fruitfulness. I wrote out the passage in a book which I used constantly, and often thought of my school as a ' garden of girls '.

As I have already confessed, I did not begin my official life with any such ideal; I followed slavishly in the tracks worn by other headmistresses who had travelled in the same direction. I had the usual large ideas about a headmistress's dignity, and, after recovering from the surprise of my appointment, I indulged in an orgy of self-gratulation, passing from my customary weak self-depreciation to a weaker self-admiration. This period is the nightmare of my retrospect, for I must have made myself thoroughly ridiculous. What is worse, I lost valuable time. I ought to have been taking my bearings and setting to work, instead of which I prinked and preened like the idiot I had suddenly become. The memory of lost opportunity is the bitterest part of retrospect—not, as might be supposed, the consciousness of failing power but of the failure to use power. " The true waste of life," said a Swedish archbishop, about the time of my retirement, " is the power we have not used and the love we

have not given." All workers in the educational vine-
yard should bear in mind that the night cometh when we
cannot work but when we can remember. Regret avails
not. There is no way of retrieving lost opportunities.
" What I have written I have written," says the Recording
Angel, and often he adds, " And may God have mercy
on your soul."

Several little happenings led me to see the folly of my
way, and served as goads to prick me out of ' the tame
paddock ' of my illusions. I remember one specially
poignant pricking. Afternoon school was over, and I was
making a tour of an almost deserted building when I
came upon a child sitting alone at detention in the second
form room. At first I was afraid she had been forgotten
by a careless form mistress but, on inquiry, found that
she was free to go as soon as she had finished a French
exercise which she was finding difficult. I wedged myself into the adjoining desk and proceeded to explain the
distinction between *son* and *le sien*. To my dismay, my
well-meant efforts had the effect of making the little
thing grow hot and nervous. I resented this inwardly
with a fierceness which surprised myself. Why, in the
name of common sense, should she be nervous in my
presence? My heart was overflowing with kindly feeling.
I took stock of the little thin figure and positively yearned
to help her, now and always. And the result was nervousness! A complete *reductio ad absurdum* if ever there was
one. I determined to set things right and, putting forth
all my stock of what might be called *charm*, I made such
headway that, when we parted outside the school gates,

she was in quite a merry mood. The first snow of winter was falling and excited us—as snow has a trick of doing with children and dogs. I stood for a moment to watch the child disappear down the hill into the snowy darkness, thinking furiously as I did so.

It was Friday evening. I chanced to be reading Herford's translation of Ibsen's *Brand* and had just finished the fourth act when I went upstairs to bed. The line, *The murky world of snow and ice* seemed an apt description of what I saw when I peered out into the darkness. The pathos of the scene in which Brand prevents Agnes from arranging the curtains so that the light of the lamp may fall on her baby's grave out in the snow, abode with me and I fell asleep only to dream of making vain efforts to rescue belated travellers who were freezing to death; of steps sinking deeper and deeper in the snow; of cries for help growing fainter and fainter. Long before dawn I woke, chill and exhausted. My waking moments were hardly less trying. I was haunted by the recollection of a French picture I had once seen, called, I believe, *Angoisses*, an unpleasantly realistic representation of a sheep bleating over her dead lamb lying prone on the frozen snow. The creature was ugly, suffering, and the whole scene disagreeable. I switched off my mind to something pleasanter, and recalled the beauty of Windermere as I had seen it a year or two ago—frozen over, with a background of snowy fells. Then I bethought me of the spring-time loveliness of the Rothay Valley, and was thinking drowsily of sheep dogs collecting their charges on the fells, when a question flashed into my mind: " Whom have you left in the snow?" It startled me into wakefulness again, and I had to be very firm with myself before I could turn my mind from snow and snowy disasters and go to sleep.

I woke in a cheerful mood and went off to spend the week-end in the pleasant society of friends outside the town, but, when I returned to my rooms on Sunday night and began my usual small preparations for the morrow's duties, depression again bore down upon me, and the question, *Whom have you left in the snow?* began to tease me once more. I stopped as I recognized a bit of rhythm about it, considered for a moment, reached down my volume of Matthew Arnold's poems, turned over the leaves vaguely, and finally came to *Rugby Chapel*, when my eye lighted on the description of

> The lonely inn 'mid the rocks
> Where the stern and taciturn host
> Stands on the threshold . . . and asks
> Whom in our party we bring?
> Whom have we left in the snow?

The question which had been haunting me was, I think, a misquotation of the last line.

I sat up late reading and rereading the poem, which seemed to be lighted up with flashes of meaning to my groping mind. I read of, and saw myself among, those

> Who eddy about
> Here and there, eat and drink,
> Chatter and love and hate,
> Striving blindly, achieving
> Nothing; and then they die,

Perish; and no one asks
Who and what they have been
More than he asks what waves,
In the moonlight solitudes mild
Of the midmost Ocean, have swelled,
Foamed for a moment and gone.

I read further of the great schoolmaster of whom the poet son writes:

But thou would'st not *alone*
Be saved, my father! *alone*
Conquer and come to thy goal,
Leaving the rest in the wild,
Therefore to thee was it given
Many *to save with thyself*
And, at the end of thy day,
O faithful shepherd, to come
Bringing thy sheep in thy hand."

Sitting there alone, I saw in a flash that my work was just that—to save others along with myself—and I chose forthwith my path to a ' clear-purposed ' goal. I had done with blind gropings and purposeless strivings. How welcome is light after darkness!

It was a strange experience and one which is as fresh in my memory as yesterday's happenings. A discouraged little schoolgirl, snow, a baby's grave in the snowy darkness, sheep, a dead lamb, vain efforts at rescue, the sound of crying—and what else? Mr. Masefield, at the end of *King Cole*, says that Molly and the juggler both felt ' a touching from beyond their ken '. That is what it seemed to me—a touching from beyond my ken.

I never forgot the lesson I had learnt. Not that I was always true to my clearly defined purpose, but I always turned back to it after failures in loyalty.

Twenty-five years later, I was in difficulties with my committee and wrote to the executive of the Head-mistresses' Association for advice. The President, to whom I was personally unknown, sent to me, as her deputy, a mutual friend who was a member of the executive. She stayed the night with me and, as we sat talking into the small hours, she, quite unaware of the inner history of my professional life, said to me, " I described you to the President as a *pastoral* headmistress." The adjective sent my thoughts flying back over the years to the snowy Sunday night when I sat with a book of poems in my hand and felt the influence of the faithful shepherd who would not " be saved alone ".

There are not wanting signposts along the road of life. I sighted one the next day when I read a letter from Elsie's mother, thanking me for having helped her with her French: it had ' heartened ' the child, she said. The word *heartened* leapt up at me and I annexed it. Later in the day, an inspector called and, in the intervals of business, confided to me his doubts about the well-being of his two daughters who were attending the high school of a certain town. " Mary," so he explained, " is the kind of girl who can get on without a teacher, but Elizabeth needs a teacher all the time." Then he added reflectively: " In my experience of schools, the girls who need attention most, get it least." Signpost number two.

When, after a long and tiring climb, we have reached

a summit, it is often possible to look back and see the little by-ways that led nowhere, turns and twists of the road which led us astray, short cuts falsely so called, morasses hidden under greenery into which we slipped unawares. I now see that the most important problem a headmistress of a municipal school has to solve is the best method of establishing and maintaining personal relationships with every child in her charge. Only thus can she be sure that all is well with the individual child. Only thus can each girl learn to trust her headmistress —to know, beyond all manner of doubt, that her headmistress will never refuse to listen to her side of the case, that effort will be recognized, practical sympathy given in the way of wise and dependable advice; that there will be no compromise on matters of principle nor any countenancing of wrong-doing. For me there was only one way of securing all this, viz. to make myself easily accessible to everyone under my control, and this I proceeded to arrange for.

(A difficulty confronts me here. The exigencies of a connected and continous narrative may lead me to convey the impression that all ideals described were reached, and that this is a record of a perfect performance. Nothing could be farther from actual fact. The ideals were formed; I kept them in view and strove to reach them, but I see myself as a faulty and floundering human being of whom it can only be said that as a whole she tried her best. Especially after the numbers in the school doubled, trebled, and quadrupled, was the doing of that best a very poor thing indeed.)

The beginning of next term found things much changed. As regards the timetable, I had handed over the advanced work in the senior classes, which had hitherto been my chief concern, and arranged to take one class a week with every form. This I found not only helpful to that mutual knowledge at which I aimed, but absolutely essential. In the event, I became the scripture specialist, teaching that subject to every child in the school who was over seven years of age. Next, as the handsome and spacious room I had hitherto occupied was somewhat recessed from the main building, I effected an exchange with the staff, and so arranged the furniture of my new quarters that, when the door stood open, the writing table at which I usually sat was out of the draught, and out of sight of passers-by in the corridor. The latter was the main corridor of the building along which the girls passed on their way to the exits and entrances and when changing classes. These rearrangements gave me a position at the hub of the building and suited my purpose perfectly. During the remaining years of my headship, that is for a quarter of a century, except for a daily twenty minutes while I drank my after-lunch coffee, I never closed that door while the school was in session, unless I was interviewing, or responding to a call for pressing administrative business. The girls all knew that by a tap at an open door they could secure my attention to whatever concerned their welfare. Many availed themselves of the opportunity, and I gained much personal knowledge of the school as the result. Even if it was only the case of a lost watch-bracelet,

I got my opportunity: the loser felt my sympathy, or sustained my rebuke for carelessness. I was no longer in any danger of being considered unapproachable. Girls—especially the earnest ones—are apt to make mountains out of molehills and I was often able in a few words to reverse that process. As time went on and we developed a good form mistress system, my work in this direction became less necessary and, in the end, I used this method chiefly as a means of checking the accounts of girls which I had heard at staff meetings, and of watching for tendencies of which I had been warned. But I never reverted to the closed door.

The policy of the open door did not suffice. Some girls never tapped at it and these were in real danger of being left out in the snow, being usually those who preferred desks in remote corners and were 'no good at games'. I should not be surprised to find that these unforthcoming girls are more numerous in municipal schools than in the high schools proper. They are hard to tackle as there is no clue as to what makes them keep in their shell. They appear to be suffering from shyness but it is not always so. If I were obliged to make a generalization on the subject of the cause of excessive reserve in girls, I should say it was a deepseated grudge against the world in general, a resentment at not being appreciated, and much self-conceit. Occasionally, indeed, I have sustained a shock in unearthing, from a very reserved child, such a colossal amount of self-conceit that I felt as though an earthworm, which I was trying to remove into a place of safety, had suddenly reared itself

and expanded into a giraffe. If such children are poor
in this world's goods, it is never safe to offer them either
practical assistance or sympathy. I am glad to know that,
even with those cases in which we seemed to make little
headway, many have outgrown their inhibitions and
developed into useful women. I remember the proud
father of a girl of this kind meeting me in the street
and telling me that his daughter—one of the toughest
cases I ever tackled—had come out top in some application
for a responsible position of, I think, welfare work. " I
can never thank you enough," he said. I accepted the
praise which I in no way deserved. One almost hopeless
case was that of a girl whose despondency was so great
that she gave me the idea of what I imagine someone
born in prison would look like. No one could do anything with her, she seemed a veritable Ishmael, until an
attack of pneumonia led to visits from her form mistress
and gifts of flowers from her form mates. Before I left
she was on the forward line in the school hockey team,
and a prominent member of the school choral. The
most successful line of treatment is to assign to them
some little posts of responsibility which, even in a school
where all such posts were voted for by the girls in the
form, may be arranged by a keen form mistress who
has ' a way with her '.

But attacks of pneumonia do not always supervene so
opportunely nor end so happily, and our failures were
more than I like to recall. I made a practice of standing
outside my door whenever the school was moving freely
about the building, and getting a word with girls who

were on my mind. Especially in the dinner hour did I find my opportunity. I remember getting hold of one such girl with a book of Liberty cretonnes out of which she chose one for my chairs—or she thought she chose it—and was quite outspoken in her delight that her choice coincided with mine. Later on in our acquaintance she made a little joke, and I knew then that she was on the way to recovery.

I did a good deal of peripatetic work of this kind, visiting class rooms casually and chatting informally with whomsoever I found an opening, always with an eye on the dark horses. Sometimes I took *Punch* with me —it was a veritable godsend, even dark horses laughed at its jokes. Laughter is good—antiseptic, a safety-valve, refreshing. One girl, by no means a dark horse, never laughed, but seemed to grow more portentously solemn as the fun waxed. Her form mistress resolved to investigate. " Nora," she said, " do you never laugh?" " Not if I can help it," was the reply. " Why on earth not?" " Well you see, if I once began, I might not be able to stop." I hasten to explain that Nora was in no wise a cynic, but a sturdy English girl who was determined to remain captain of her emotions as she was of the school hockey team. Another trick was to take, generally on Mondays, the book I had been reading during the week-end, show it to the girls and tell them in the space of a minute or so my ideas about it, even leaving it for them to copy out a quotation or look at a picture. (I wonder if all schoolgirls are as fond of quotations as were the Snellham girls.) I remember their fascinated interest in the potter verses in *Omar*, and their copying out the picturesque proverb on the title page of Margot Asquith's autobiography—*Les chiens aboyent, la caravane passe*. Another wrote out a sentence from the second volume of the Life of Walter Hines Page about its number of healthy and happy citizens being the true wealth of a nation. One by-product of this casual intercourse was that a few girls began to take an interest in the kind of book I showed them. I consider that there is nothing harder to compass than the inducing of a habit of good reading in the pupils of a municipal school. An ounce of practice is worth a pound of precept, and the actual handling of such books of travel, biography, *belles lettres*, &c., did actually kindle the sacred flame in the hearts of some. This I found out much later from conversation with my ' old girls '. If I were told that the down from the breast of the mother bird kept the nursling warmer than any other, I should incline to believe it.

Looking back on this part of my work, I see myself as heavily platitudinous, and squirm as I realize the fact. I am easily bored by platitudes, and it is a blow to my self-esteem to be obliged to own to a constant use of them. My consolation lies in the thought that what is platitude to the adult may be fresh truth to the adolescent, and that time cannot undo what once was true. When does a truth become a platitude? Does this process of degeneration depend upon the utterer?—or on the hearer? I am sure that tags have their uses. Tennyson says that

> Truth embodied in a tale
> Shall enter in at lowly doors.

Truth embodied in a *tag* sometimes finds entrance into the youthful mind in virtue of its brevity. With platitudes one must be very careful when dealing with girls at all stages of development. With some, the commonplace must be avoided at all costs, and long-windedness is always fatal. What is usually safe is the terse and epigrammatic, and blessed is the headmistress who is gifted with a sense of quick humour. Heavy humour is worse than none.

I tried to analyse the effect of my speeches and was enabled to do so because some of my ' old girls ' were fond of alluding to them. The result of inquiries was not always gratifying to my *amour-propre*. One girl said that what she remembered best was the advice, ' Never be afraid of water whether inside or out '. I had a bad attack of squirming and forebore to probe farther. Later the spontaneous confession of one of the ' old girls ' delighted me. It would seem that I was pointing out the ambiguity of the line:

A little dry old man without a star

(which occurs in the description of King Gama in Tennyson's poem *The Princess*), and explaining that the words might mean either that the old king had not a ' riband to stick in his coat ' or that his personality lacked radiance. She said I referred them to Matthew Arnold's sonnet, and quoted the lines:

O human soul, as long as thou canst so
Set up a mark of everlasting light
Above the howling senses' ebb and flow, &c.,

and that the idea of spiritual radiance had never left her. I rejoiced over this—water never fired immortal soul but spiritual radiance may set a world a-glow. One thing became clear to me: it is impossible to calculate the effect of words on the eager adolescent mind. It does not depend on the speaker or on the hearer, but on both with, perhaps, a ' touching from beyond our ken '.

Home environment has an immense influence on a girl's progress at school—I did not need the disclosures of modern psychology to convince me of this truth. I soon felt it to be of paramount importance to effect closer relationships with the parents of my girls. Open days did little to assist in this direction as many of the parents were too busy to come. I found out that they liked coming to ' have a talk ' about their children's progress and that, in that way, I could find out what I wanted to know. I made access both to the building, and to myself personally, as easy as possible by seeing to it that the front door, which was about three yards from my room, was kept open except when I was teaching. Thus it became the rule—not so much abused as my staff and friends predicted it would be—for parents, whose time did not allow of their making appointments, to walk in, with as little ceremony as might be, and have a chat about things that were on their minds. The arrangement answered well and saved my time in the end, in as much as I ceased to have ' complaints ' in letters which needed personal attention. True—that I was at everyone's beck and call and often fell a prey to a fussy parent. On the other hand the school was not misunderstood as so often is the case when parents have to depend on second-hand information about its doings. *Tout comprendre c'est tout pardonner*. I recognize the right of the parents of pupils in municipal schools to the fullest information about the organization, results, rules, &c., of the school. I published a year-book setting forth all such details, and these personal interviews were for the individual. I am not without hope that I was sometimes able to get a word in with a cantankerous father (nothing makes a girl so ' nervy ' as a bad-tempered father) or a careless mother. It is one of the worst signs of the times that nowadays women undertake ' the high emprise of motherhood ' with less sense of responsibility than before the war. Not a few of the applicants for admission to the Preparatory were scarred in mind, or body, or both, by careless mothering. On the other hand, the over-parented child suffers. The golden mean in parental relationships is rarely attained.

Although the system of self-discipline which we ultimately evolved did excellent work, and the supplementary one of advisory form mistressing made for personal interest in the girls, I felt that the delegating of my share in the latter was a loss to me. A grip on the school can be gained in no other way. *In no other way can a head feel sure of her school*. For this reason, I deprecate the building of schools for very large numbers of girls—boys do not, perhaps, need the personal touch as much as girls—and, in my case, I felt that four hundred was the maximum number of pupils whose names I could remember and whose personality I could appreciate.

When I had to delegate, I preferred to do so in the upper school. I incline to think the headmistress is most needed in the first and second years: the newcomers need to be reassured; to be guided into a sympathetic understanding with the aims and discipline of the school; to be led into a happy feeling of proprietorship with regard to it, which later develops into pride in, and loyalty to, it. This achieved, good work follows almost as a matter of course. Amid all the pother of fees, entrance forms, health records, classifications, schedules, interviews, and the rest that marks the beginning of a new session, I kept to the end a feeling of excitement as I watched the new girls, reduced to a superficial uniformity in their gym tunics, filing along our spacious corridors, and I was able to review the latest recruits to my regiment of miniature women.

But there was another result of my policy of the open door which delighted me more than all the rest put together. The girls took me for granted—as far as a headmistress can be so taken. By this, I mean that they were at ease in my presence; few were nervous with me. I was by no means an easy-going headmistress; when I said, "This must cease," it ceased forthwith—but, for all that, with few exceptions, the girls did not fear me and my rule was on easy terms. I had a droll, if belated, reassurance of my success in this direction. In pursuance of my policy of paying great attention to the forms of fresh entrants, I had undertaken to coach a large form of eleven-year-olds in form dramatics, and was sitting at the desk in their room, surrounded by the thirty

odd girls to whom I was assigning parts in the plays.
In our form dramatics every girl had a part, and there
was much excited discussion about suitability of stature,
voice, colouring, &c. We needed, I remember, two kings
and queens, a fairy godmother, a Prince Charming, a
goddess, a witch, a dwarf, a beggar-girl, street urchins,
singers, dancers, courtiers and so forth. The child
standing close to me on my left began to feel anxious
lest she, not being in my direct line of vision, should
be forgotten in the distribution. Presently, I was aware
of a thin arm laid across the back of my neck, then of a
faint pressure from it. I went on as though unconscious,
and, in a minute or two, she shook my shoulder gently
once, and again a second time, quite firmly. Then—
I felt certain that what I had hoped for had been granted
to me. I had known I was trusted: now I realized that
my rule inspired no fear. For, if you are afraid of a headmistress, you do not shake her any more than you would
tweak the tail of a dog whose bite is as bad as his bark.

If I were to describe how delighted I was about this, I
should expose myself to a charge of sentimental exaggera-
tion. I had come within measurable distance of realizing
one of my ideals and, being as a whole unsuccessful in that
respect—must a man's reach *always* exceed his grasp?
does the road wind uphill *all* the way?—I was propor-
tionately glad about it. If I had been Handel, I should
probably have exploded into a Hallelujah Chorus; if I
had been Pippa, I should have gone round lilting about
' the lark on the wing '; if I had been a street urchin,
I might have turned a surprising series of somersaults.

As I was plain Marion Cleeve, I betook my prim person
to the comparative seclusion of my room, sat down,
laughed a good deal and cried a little.

During the interval between my resignation and my
retirement, I heard many opinions expressed about this
part of our work. (I say *our* because by that time I was
backed by a zealous staff whose ideals were in the same
direction.) The father of a sixth form girl came to see
me and, after explaining that he had never ' set eyes on '
me before—I was by way of being a recluse—remarked
that he thought the influence of my school was unlike
anything he had ever come across. " I shouldn't say
it was exactly maternal, and yet it *is* maternal; I shouldn't
say it was exactly spiritual (did he mean religious, I
wonder) and yet it *is* spiritual." Then, looking at me
rather as though I were a conjurer, he added, " I should
like to know how it's done." I made no attempt at
explanation and he went off murmuring something
which I did not quite hear and which contained the words
prayer and fasting. If he was making a generalization
about the source of all good influence—ascribing it to
reliance on a Power higher than ourselves as typified
by *prayer*, and selflessness as typified by *fasting*—he
was right. It is here that we must look for the secret of
the spiritual force of the great saints of history, and
the more complete the reliance, the greater the selflessness,
the more victorious the force. In my own pettifogging
way, I found this to be the case. When I allowed impatience, fatigue, resentment, or any other form of selfish-
ness to come between me and my school or to interfere

with my attitude to any child—*then* I was feeble. When I saw and followed I was effective. Writes the poet:

> I have always had one lode-star; now
> As I look back, I see that I have wasted
> Or progressed, as I looked toward that star.

Thus was it with me.

The sweetest bit of praise—a bit which I cuddle to myself and think of over and over again—came from an ' old girl ' who had married a medical missionary and was on the eve of departure for the mission field. " I have told my husband," she said, " that we need not worry about our children. We can send them home and they will be sent to this school where *no little lonely girls are overlooked*." I believe there is a spiritual force which is invincible. I have seen something like it exerted and triumphant, and traced its effect in the story of the progress of mankind. Yet this chapter must close on a note of failure—failure to overcome by that spiritual force available for all, one of those obstacles which ever and anon check the currents of influence. The incident is a typical one in my experience. There were two sisters in the school who came from a good home, were well endowed physically and mentally and marked out for a happy and successful school career. Something went awry and the girls suffered. They never fell in with the others, made few friends, were never elected to any of the little posts of honour, and later began to be ailing in a way which I had learnt to recognize as marking a lack of inner harmony. The cause was ascertained. A delicate and captious mother full and fond of grievances had prejudiced her children in some important ways by injudicious criticism. It is fatally easy to do this: a single remark suffices. I came to know this, but took no steps to set things right, allowing resentment and fear of misunderstanding to come between me and the cause. The children were the losers for, if you are born into a cat's cradle, you are bound to develop a cat's tricks, and only the grace of God avails to save you from the arched back and stiffened tail.

CHAPTER IV

Discipline: the Assistant Staff

The connotation of the word *discipline* may be so extended as to include almost every subject discussed in this book. Discipline goes down to the very roots of educational method and determines what manner of fruit a school shall yield. What I shall record under this heading will include not only my experiences, but also the opinions I have formed since I ceased to be a disciplinarian. *Il y a toujours ceux qui font leurs beaux discours sur l'escalier* and I am one of them.

The assistant staff are closely associated with discipline in its widest significance: the head may supply the power, the assistants work the machine.

When I began my life as headmistress, the school contained about eighty girls and five mistresses, some of the latter being about my own age. As the town was dull, we found little to interest us outside the school, and we associated as chums, both figuratively and literally playing our games together. Well do I remember certain Friday evenings when, my housekeeper having been given leave of absence, my staff, who all lived in more or less uncomfortable lodgings, used to take possession of my kitchen and do their week-end cooking. One evening, we had a pastry-making competition in which I scored highest in a maiden effort with a pasty so light that it had to be eaten forthwith. This magnificent *tour de force* was, I am convinced, the result of complete dependence on mother-wit or the subconscious—are they not the same thing?—for my methods were such as to agitate the orthodox, being described as *slapdash*, and, by a witty Anglo-French mistress, as due to *legerdemain*.

Few headmistresses retain either the lightheartedness or the leisure for such frolics as we enjoyed at that time. The school, as it grew in numbers and range, absorbed me body and soul, leaving me with neither energy nor leisure. The war made things very hard: it took from me three or four of the ablest members of my staff whose record of fine service in the school amounted in the aggregate to fifty years. Then I came to know what worry was like. At the time there was a great dearth of teachers, and once I had to engage three additional staff at very short notice, my advertisement bringing only eight applications for the three posts. Two of these appointed proved misfits; the third, a geography specialist, a valuable asset. Numbers went up by leaps and bounds and, as the excellent teaching of the staff I had lost had resulted in our gaining early recognition as an advanced course school, I was hard put to it to secure successors to carry on the work. An advertisement for a highly qualified science specialist brought only two applications, both without experience. The statement in one of the scanty testimonials that the holder had ' a truly scientific

mind ' was encouraging enough to send me speeding off
to the neighbouring university town, at which she was
just completing her diploma year. I awaited her in the
Common Room; she entered; I scanned her from head to
foot, noting her well-brushed hair and neat blouse, and
inwardly ejaculating, " Thank heaven, she's clean," I
engaged her there and then. In the train on the return
journey I became a prey to misgivings. What if the girls
didn't take to her? She was so immature and, like myself,
looked a greater fool than she was. I resolved desperately
to take the Science Sixth into my confidence. Closing
the form room door carefully behind me, I confronted
the half-dozen tall, capable girls of the upper division
of the form and spoke somewhat as follows: " I have
engaged Miss X to teach you science. She is clever,
young and inexperienced—in fact, in the exact position
in which you expect to find yourselves in a few years.
She possesses the knowledge you need. It is up to you
to get that knowledge from her, and for that reason it
behoves you to help her to impart it by every means in
your power." The result was droll. When they saw what
she was like, they took possession of her, treated her with
maternal indulgence, saw to it that she held her own with
the laboratory assistant and that the apparatus cupboards
were kept neat. This was effected only by dint of much
admonition. One day I overheard one of them scolding
her and telling her not ' to muddle things up so '. I
glanced anxiously at the culprit, but saw no sign of resentment as she hurried to do as she was told. When the
science side developed and she had to teach large classes,

she was not a success, but some of her pupils in the advanced course won distinction in her subject. In her letters after she left, she referred to the happy times she had had with the Sixth, ' who always seemed to be older than I was '. Later I learnt that a headmistress, whose committee had refused to appoint Miss X as being too immature, failed to keep her examination science going for lack of a teacher. The times were indeed very hard: emergency appointments are apt to prove misfits. I was comparatively fortunate, as the instrument of government of the school assigned to the head the " sole right of appointment " of staff. This made prompt action possible and saved the situation.

That heads of schools should have the sole right of appointing staff seems to me the only way of making him or her responsible for the school. There can be no such thing as a divided responsibility: if you try to divide responsibility, it collapses like a meringue which you are trying to cut in two. It is true that a headmistress may so influence an unsatisfactory member of staff that she may cease to be unsatisfactory, but this is expecting too much. The workman is the best judge of his own tools, and should not be required to mend the same before he can set to work. It is impossible for the inexpert in the science and art of school-keeping to appreciate the delicate distinction between, let us say, the kind of mistress who is required to play the double part of form mistress and specialist, and the specialist pure and simple. Also, with many committees, as undoubtedly with the Snellham one (to many of whose members the exercise of patronage was as the breath of life) it goes against the grain to allow the head the *virtual* decision, while retaining the nominal right of choice. In other words, the committee has its way, whatever the nature of the arrangement for joint consultation.

It is one of the difficulties of municipally controlled education that the vulgar mind does not realize that expert knowledge is needed in educational administration. A little knowledge will always prove a danger to those who come in contact with it, for the fewer ideas a man has, the more tenaciously does he cling to them. If there is one thing more important than another in regard to municipal schools, it is the careful adaptation of the school to the town, to the type of girl, to the aims and ambitions of the parents. It took me some time to discover in what direction my school was likely to excel, and to organize to give its genius scope, and I was fortunate in being left unmolested during that responsible time. For schools need self-expression as well as individuals, something to be proud of in the school makes for tradition and loyalty. It is easy to read glowing accounts of the doings of other schools and let zeal outrun discretion, in which case a monotonous mediocrity will probably be the distinguishing feature of the school. A municipal headmistress must never fail in what she attempts. If she is to be a successful leader, trust in her judgment must be complete. How hard it is for outsiders to realize all this, I soon found out. A governor once urged upon me the appointment of an inexperienced singing master and justified his interference by asking:

" Do you realize that when I was a young man (thirty or forty years ago) I used often to stand up on a platform and sing solos?" He was a cycle dealer and I had to choke back a rejoinder that when I was young I rode a bicycle.

The ideal arrangement for the appointment of staff is for the governors to have the right of confirmation of the Head's appointment, thus securing the right of veto, but no right of interference in the actual selection. The result of such a veto would be open discussion, which is desirable in all municipal affairs. Secrecy breeds suspicion and affords opportunity for the unscrupulous. For that reason I think that all resignations should be made to the governors and, after consideration of a report from the Head, all dismissals should come direct from them. Again, open discussion within the bounds of the committee room would result. It is a temptation to a headmaster or mistress to condone bad work rather than face the odium of being considered a martinet, and I have heard it said that no Head of a vigorous school escapes it. It is to the credit of the human heart to incline to the side of the under dog; it is to the discredit of human intelligence not to discern which is the under, and which the top, dog.

But, whatever the procedure, the duty of cutting one's losses in regard to inefficient staff must be faced, for poor teaching in any part of the school injures those who are being prepared for careers of different kinds. I should encourage all agencies which defend the professional status of the teacher and seek for security of tenure. But for the head of a school to allow a poor teacher to settle down in a school is a crime against both staff and pupils. Perfunctory and dull teaching create a prejudice against things of the mind. Do children ever rid themselves of an aversion from a subject which was taught dully and without enthusiasm? The ideal teacher is a radiator who diffuses the warmth of enthusiasm and the light of knowledge. Teachers must *glow*. A glow attracts like nothing else in this cold dark world. The mere sound of the word makes us think of glowing embers of the hearth when we draw aside the curtains and peer into the chill darkness outside; of distant lamplight shining from cottage windows on the distant hillside; of the brazier in the roadmaker's hut; of camp fires with dimly-outlined figures gathered around. There are more kinds of glow than one. " Did not our heart burn within us as He talked by the way, and while He opened to us the Scriptures?" said the two disciples who, on the world's first Easter day, walked alongside the world's greatest Teacher on the way to Emmaus. Such a glow is what the world needs, for it brings all others along with it. My heart leapt up in response to Mr. Ramsay MacDonald when, as premier, he proclaimed his ideal to be a fireside for every man. That is what all the coal trouble is about—not coal itself, but that the glow imprisoned in the heart of the coal may be released for wife, child, and wage-earning father to gather round at nightfall, none making them afraid. The education problem will be solved when all teachers have a glow at the centre, and release it to warm their pupils. It is up to teachers to set the world aglow, and within their power to do so.

My imagination—which is sometimes a help and at other times a snare—has ample time, here in the peace of my Innisfree, for playing round the topics I am discussing. This evening, I have been wandering up and down these gentle slopes and picturing to myself the kind of headmistress I should like to serve under, if I had to begin my professional life again as an assistant mistress. Inevitably memory reverted to the personalities of the heads of my first two schools. One, who in private often addressed me as ' my dear child ', almost killed me in a few months with a multiplicity of mark lists, records, reports, and such-like lumber. The second, who was ' a jolly good fellow ', lost no opportunity of shifting her duties on to other people's shoulders. I had a nervous breakdown under the first and recuperated under the second. I came to the conclusion that the quality I should most value in my headmistress would be *trustworthiness*. If I could rely on her justice and her judgment, she might box my ears now and again, if it relieved her feelings. I don't mind a bit of temper provided it's not of the kind described as *uncertain*. (There is nothing more nerve-racking than working with anyone whose explosions are unpredictable.) My ideal must, therefore, be free from prejudice and able to view matters impersonally. Neither must she be a muddler. She must be incapable of dumping down in my second year chemistry class newcomers who have never before seen the inside of a laboratory. I must also know that she is not the kind to drop a subject out of the curriculum for a term or two because she can't fit it into the timetable, and reinstate it at the end of that time because she finds that she can, being under the impression that the loss of so many lessons will not make any difference in, what she vaguely calls, ' the long run '. She must be able so to manage her promotions that the B forms are not like the goods at a rummage sale—at all stages of dilapidation. By all means she must have the calm courage that stands firm in defence of professional principle, however governors rage and parents imagine a vain thing, and that great gift of a sincerity so deep that you are sure that the unfavourable criticism she has just made on your work is a genuine desire to right the wrong, and not a mere pressure of the thumb of authority, or a wanton tug at the bit and bridle. She must keep on her pedestal (I should detest a free and easy chief) and be a leader that leads. Her eyes will be steadfast and her gaze direct. (I pray kind heaven that she be not spectacled.) She will smile not constantly but with a quick spontaneity. Her normal expression may have a touch of sternness about it, for she views life steadily and sees it whole, and I will not allow her to wear even rose-coloured spectacles. I trust she may not be tactful, over-tactful I mean, for I have that mistrust of tact which comes from myself often having taken cover behind that virtue ' inclining to a defect '. All headmistresses know the force of the temptation to prophesy smooth things, to praise what is not praiseworthy, to write unduly favourable reports, and to cover up the entire unworthy proceeding by

referring to it as ' the exercise of a little tact '. No! my
ideal will face up bravely to things as they are. For tact
at best is only an interim virtue, a temporary makeshift.
When this imperfect world is perfected, when the shadows
flee away and we see clearly—then, we shall look steadily
at one another and speak the simple truth in love. Of
course, she will be all a-glow: firstly, because her heart
is very pitiful, and secondly, because she is keenly alive
to the charm of knowledge, of work for the joy of the
working, and passionately convinced of the happiness of
the strenuous life. How I should delight in hearing her
praised! not as merely brilliant or charming. I should
wish that people who were discussing her and her work
should exclaim, " How *fine* she is!" Then should I
answer, " Yes, indeed—fine and *re*fined," and, proudly
quoting Browning's lover, ask, " Is she not pure gold
my mistress?"

(How is it that we admire most the virtues we lack? I
oozed tact, and was spectacled.)

Several years ago, I was travelling back from the
annual meeting of the Headmistresses' Association, in
a railway carriage specially reserved. As the meeting
had been in London, several of us had availed ourselves
of the opportunity to interview applicants for vacancies
on our staffs, and we fell to comparing notes. We agreed
as to the inadequacy of such brief interviews and vented
our spleen over the incompleteness of testimonials, one
pessimist declaring that she had been buying ' a pig in
a poke '. In the general discussion that followed, someone asked for an expression of opinion as to the relative

importance of the following qualifications of assistant mistresses: *Outstanding and desirable personality, academic honours, teaching gift.* If we were sure of only one, which should we choose? A short argument followed as to the connotation of the word *personality.* We agreed that it should cover *physique, mentality,* and *principles.* A general agreement was soon reached that academic honours—these were pre-advanced-course days—were the least important, and that teaching gift was the rarest. The voting went in favour of personality, I being the only one who stood for teaching gift. As a matter of experience, I have always recognized the paramount importance of teaching gift. First, because I believe dull teaching to be one of the two main causes of the failure of English education to attract; second, because I believe that knowledge, and the process of acquiring it, has a beneficial effect upon character; third, because I feel that defective personality can be most easily supplemented by other agencies and that the prime duty of a teacher is to teach. In other words, a teacher fails if she is not a power in the class room. I therefore stifled my longings for good looks and general attractiveness when I felt sure they did not accompany the teaching gift. As an inspector who was expressing surprise at the work and general outlook of a very pretty girl, once remarked to me: " Beauty, brains, and intellectual keenness are seldom found in combination."

The result of this emphasis on teaching gift was that my staff generally came out strong at Full Inspections, being described as above the average in teaching ability.

As long as fortune favoured me in this respect, the school prospered in the way I most valued. " The Snellham girls learn of their own accord," said a diploma student who was practising in my school. I was pleased at this spontaneous remark, because I believe that it is natural for children to enjoy the process of acquiring knowledge, and that bad teaching dulls this faculty of joyous learning, and permanently injures mentality. When all teachers are good teachers—that is, when all teachers teach *con amore*—then all children will learn *con amore*. It is the *glow* that does the trick. In the higher sphere of human activity, is there ever any successful work which is not ' work for the joy of the working '?

When we get to bed-rock, a teacher's task is to induce the young of the human species to put forth effort in the higher part of his make-up corresponding to his instinctive conations in the lower. We stress the importance of pleasurable emotion in the latter case, and neglect it in the former. I know it was a humorist who said, " It doesn't matter what you teach a boy, provided he doesn't like it." There is, however, a grave irony in the dictum: it would almost appear to have been our principle of action. The general assumption is that lessons are dull proceedings and the boy or girl who enjoys them is a marked character.

The blame lies with both teachers and curriculum. Good teachers are born, not made, for without a certain faculty of sympathetic insight and a degree of native mental alertness, no one can develop into a first-rate teacher. They may be purveyors of information, but not teachers. A natural teacher instructs himself as he goes along, learning the tricks of his trade by practice, prompted by intuition and directed by insight into the minds of his pupils. I was always interested in a skilful use of the art of questioning, which, at its best, is so inspiringly effective and, at its worst, painfully tedious in its long-drawn-out processes. A clever teacher will learn by experience how to extract correct answers from dullards, without boring the whole class in the process, and it is a fine triumph of pedagogic skill when, by the rearrangement of the form of the question, simplifying, shifting the ground a little, and so on, dull wits may be roused into activity, and the whole class become interested in what may easily have developed into an exercise in deductive reasoning. A vigorous drill in the short quick answering to brief, pertinent questions will rouse a class on a sultry after-noon, and a sudden call to write answers to such ques-tions be as effective as a call to attention. I retain a delightful memory of a French mistress who, while dealing with individuals in her translation classes, succeeded in keeping the rest of the class interested in the reading and not a few of them critically alert. She would rap out such questions and comments as the following: " Yes, *nœud* does mean *knot*, but we prefer a figurative meaning. Yes, *difficulty* would do, but there's a little Shakesperian word that would fit in exactly? Yes, *rub* is the best word for this context." This popular and successful teacher made a practice of repeating each answer so that no one lost the thread of the discussions, and, instead of naming each girl as she addressed her, she moved quickly and lightly in her direction. She justified the use of such a fatiguing manœuvre as economy of effort, ' because I hear all they say and don't have to remember names '.

But, although such powers as I have indicated are innate in a ' born teacher ', there still remains a kind of knack about the art of teaching, and knacks may be acquired. The word *knack* interests me: it is curiously onomatopœic. A knack is something quick, strong, effective—like the sound of the word. It is not a dodge and not a fluke, but has a bit of both about it. When you have got it—whether it is the knack of double-declutching in gear-changing, or in managing a rowdy middle-school form—you wonder why you ever found it difficult. None the less, when you are trying to explain how it's done, you end by saying, " It's a knack and you have to find it out for yourself."

From the beginning of my headmistressing, I made a point of keeping all the discipline in my own hands, and for many years the only punishment was being reported to the Head. I had two reasons for this procedure. First, I wanted to know what was going on in the delicate matter of punitive disciplining, and secondly, I wanted to shield my staff from the odium incurred sometimes as the result of punishing girls. Mistresses differ much in their success in this respect. Some need no such assistance in discipline. Those who do need it either face or shirk the obligation of inflicting punishment—the former being usually the salt of the profession. They nerve them-selves for the performance of a painful duty, and thereby lose that surface popularity which the easy-going often absorb. I was determined that honour should go to the faithful, and the only way to effect this was to assume the onus of punishment myself. Municipal schools are bound to allow the right of free criticism to rate-paying parents, and this arrangement focused it on me. I feel that this is only fair: the brunt of the battle is fought in the class room, and it is up to the Head to clear the ground for action. I was anxious that my staff should be approved outside the school and, in wholesome fashion, beloved inside. Moreover, I did not want to be a pedagogic Duke of Plaza Toro, of whom the witty librettist writes that he

> Led his regiment from behind:
> He found it less exciting.

There is no wisdom in trying to avoid the inevitable. A headmistress is responsible for everything under her control—whether a mistress forgets herself so far as to call a child a duffer, or the kitchen maid does not conscientiously gouge out the eyes of the dinner potatoes.

I used to wonder sometimes whether training colleges paid enough attention to the details of class management. I was reading an article the other day which warned motorists in traffic from expecting cyclists, pedestrians or sheep to do the ' sensible thing '. It is sometimes wise to expect folly. I found young mistresses repeatedly indifferent to such details as seeing that the class was supplied with all requisites (pencils, scribbler, apparatus), to the style of blackboard writing, to evenness of enunciation—very important in large classes—to emphasis on the tricky points of the lesson, to the repetition of key sentences, fresh words and so forth. Ninety-nine per cent of the cases I had to deal with were reported for inattention in class due to neglect of such simple matters as I have just enumerated. " Miss Cleeve, Joan sneezed just as Miss X said the word *carbohydrate* which I had never heard before. I nudged Mary to let me see what she had written, and she thought I was up to fun, but, *in the beginning*, I was only trying to keep up." A girl fumbling for a metric ruler has been known to miss the announcement of the subject of a lesson and to remain ignorant of it throughout. My lengthy experience in dealing with such cases enables me to dogmatize on the subject. The faculty of discriminating the essential, of going to the heart of a subject without circumlocution, of realizing where the child mind may fail to follow, and fortifying that exact spot by emphasis and repetition is the basis of effective teaching.

Teachers fresh from training colleges *invariably* lecture their classes, and when, as happens inevitably, the attention becomes overstrained they fall back on the dictation of notes. The *dictation* of notes is the *pis-aller* of the incapable teacher and is justifiable only under pressure of examination preparation. A still more serious habit of ex-training college students is the neglect of the use of textbooks. I have traced the heresy that a lesson which dispenses with the aid of a textbook is the ideal lesson. Never was there a more serious error. Textbooks nowadays are very different from the cram books of our school days, and to ' get up ' a lesson based on some of these newer publications is an aid to inducing the habit of good reading. A boy or girl who has done a course of middle school history based on a well-written history textbook will retain a more orderly recollection of the sequence of events and be much more interested than if he had been forced to spend time in copious note-taking, punctuated by intervals of lecturing. Surely the partial success of the Dalton Plan should have taught us so much, as well as the advantage of providing the class with syllabuses of work to be done, monthly, terminally, and sessionally. To teach the use of books is part of the duty of municipal schools, whose pupils come so often from homes where books are not familiar friends but merely *habitués* of the solitary bookcase. The schools that send out young people with a taste for good literature are successful in a very special sense. I am not sure that English philistinism is on the decrease.

While I have been writing this chapter I have recalled with feelings of the deepest gratitude the many devoted and clever co-workers I had on my staff. Especially, perhaps, the form mistresses, who, in a municipal school, play an all-important part. A good form mistress *must* be a good woman: no self-seeker could ever make a success of form-mistressing. She is sure to be a gifted woman—a charming compound of teacher, counsellor, comrade, with a touch of the maternal. (If I were a man, I should try to induce a successful form mistress to marry me.) Her work, glorified by self-sacrifice, is a fine sublimation of instinct, and measureless in its influence.   Of form-mistressing, I am sure it is true that ' there shall never be one lost good '.

My recollections of staffs and staffing extend back to a time when the Burnham scale was not so much as thought of—when we were all ill-paid.   I remember when the purchase of a new costume was an excitement for the whole staff room and the mere mention of a silk lining thereto, a thrill.   How different the outlook now!

But disquieting rumours reach me.   I am anxious to avoid the weakness of senility, but I sometimes wonder whether dignity and devotion have not gone out with dowdiness.   I hear of young teachers who are ashamed of their high calling, and of those who try to ape the fashionably frivolous.   Teachers have been successful in securing for themselves better conditions of life and wider opportunities and are to be much congratulated.   But— *nothing fails like success*.

CHAPTER V

Systems of Discipline

My Innisfree is not looking its best this morning. The torrential rainfall of last night has ceased, but the plants and flowers under my windows were hard hit by the heavy showers. Sweet-peas sag, hollyhocks have lost their upright bearing, soiled rose-leaves lie about and even the massive marigolds are dishevelled. Clouds lower and everything drips dully. I feel out of sorts, aggrieved, and impatient for the sun to show himself and hearten all that droops and draggles.

A little reflection leads me to realize that my resentment is unreasonable: that I have forgotten the pit from which I was but lately digged—in other words the barrenness of my early environment at Snellham. There, I should have been thankful for even such a rain-bedraggled garden patch as the one before me. I call to mind that longing for natural beauty which grew almost unbearable when spring was in the air and every moment ought to have been ' sweeter than before '. On Saturdays, before I grew resigned, I used to take tram or train and journey through miles of grimy country, in search of an early larch wood or primroses on banks. At Easter and Whitsuntide, I sped farther on similar quests. One may measure the intensity of a longing by the intensity of disappointment at delay in its satisfaction. A grudge lingers in my mind against Fontainebleau for failing me at Easter. There was no reason for anticipating a belated bourgeoning; yet, when I drew up my blinds the morning after a late arrival—barely a tree in leaf! The New Forest was up - to - date, and at Whitsuntide the Lake District never disappointed me. True, the rain fell oft but gently; but flowers of gorgeous colouring rioted in soul-satisfying profusion near Fox How and along the Rothay valley, where the deep, quiet joy of being in the midst of such loveliness was enhanced by the thought of the noble living and high thinking of

> Souls tempered with fire,
> Fervent, heroic and good,
> Helpers and friends of mankind.

For there are visions about in those parts and white Presences on the Fells.

It was this thirst for greenery that, in the early years of my sojourn in Snellham, led me to try to rear window plants and, failing actual blooms, to cherish—an aspidistra. I am timid about making such an admission and hasten to explain that, at that remote time, aspidistras had not lost their social prestige. I hope that even if they had, I should have been true to a plant which, in its own curving, blade-like fashion, may lay claim, at least, to the beauty of glossy greenery and, when it is reared as carefully as mine was, to a fine symmetrical setting. I am prejudiced in favour of what is easily obtainable, the possession of which rouses no pangs of envy. I am thankful for the fragile and tremulous beauty of wild flowers and grieve that they are so short-lived. The colour shading of some wild roses is unsurpassed, passing as it does from the hesitancy of palest pink to a crimson intensity. A harebell is hard to beat for shy grace, and a wayside wood carpeted with bluebells is one of my favourite objects in idle thought.

When I bought my aspidistra for one and fourpence from a stall in the Snellham market, I was living in rooms which looked directly on the street. I placed it at my window, and somewhat to my dismay, it became an object of such interest to the neighbourhood that, one day, I was surprised by a gift from a friendly vanman (who called daily with provisions and was, I believe, related in some avuncular or fraternal way to the school) of what he called a ' lard bucket ' painted a conscientious green. Hitherto I had not connected lard with buckets— I believe subconsciously I had hoped for higher things for lard—and I much preferred flower pots *au naturel*. I judged, however, that the Snellhamites in that part of the town abhorred the *au naturel*, not subscribing to the dictum that ' beauty unadorned is adorned the most '. So I accepted with thanks, and henceforth my aspidistra led a still more public life enthroned in the lard bucket. It flourished exceedingly and, when I parted from it, had forty full-grown leaves to its credit.

There is much natural law in the spiritual world. I have a trick of attaching mystical meanings to things that move, sound, happen. A kind of analogy seemed to exist between my experiences with my aspidistra and my disciplinary efforts with my girls. At first, my plant suffered from overmuch attention, and so did my girls. I was always too anxious about my school. Aspidistras, like the Snellham girls, are sturdily independent: they prefer to be left to struggle upwards and onwards un-aided and to manage their own concerns. When I for-mulated my first disciplinary schemes, I did not allow scope for free development. Also, hoping to secure the most symmetrical setting for my plant, I used to tie up the heavy straggling leaves. With the same intention did I tie up my pupils with rules and regulations. I used to wash the leaves of the plant until I bethought me to take it out of doors and allow soft showers to cleanse and refresh it. By and by, I ceased to tie its leaves up, but turned it round for the sun to lure the growing stems in the right direction. Ultimately my school discipline resolved itself into something the same. I threw my whole strength into making the best possible arrange-ments for all things bright and beautiful to act on the life of the school, to draw my girls upward and onward and strengthen them for the climbing. That done, I stood aside for Nature and the Holy Spirit of God to do the rest.

This, I believe, is the true discipline. Whom the Lord loveth He chasteneth (Moffatt's version—*disciplineth*) and all things work together for good to them that love God. There is the discipline, and there its method. The connotation of the word has changed since I began my gropings after the ideal method. Once it was dangerously near being synonymous with chastisement; now, when punishment, strictly so called, has become the *pis-aller* of authority, its meaning is more akin to *nurture*, because it includes all the influences brought to bear on the learner (or disciple) for his edification. Our Lord was disciplining Peter, James, and John when, on the Mount of Transfiguration, He caused them to behold His glory; He was disciplining them when, on the descent, they met the scuffling baffled crowd, and heard Him deal with that most perplexing of human miseries—a suffering child. Not always the gleaming hill-tops, not always the quag-mires, of human experience. Was there no disciplinary training during the storm on the lake? In His walking over the dark waters? When He said of the belated, hungry crowd, " Give *ye* them to eat "? When He insisted on washing Peter's feet, and asked him thrice, " Simon, son of John, lovest thou me?" " I am glad," said Jesus, referring to Lazarus's death, " that I was not there, *to the intent that ye may believe.*"

In feeling my way to a complete system of self-govern-ment, I made little use of punishment. I approve of punishment wisely administered and am not able to endorse all that the sentimentalists have to say about the baleful effect of fear—a subject in the treatment of which I think I detect some confusion of thought. The fear from which there is no possibility of escape is deadening. The fear which rouses to action is surely an evolutionary necessity having its counterpart in the spiritual process. That an idle boy should be afraid of his father if he takes home a bad report is salutary, may lead to greater effort and even to the formation of the habit of strenuousness. If, however, the boy has done his best, is incapable of greater effort, then the fear of consequences will have a paralysing effect, and bad become worse. Few incentives to effort are harmful to the young—that is, to those capable of further development. Sloth and slackness, which bring along with them the self-indulgence which kills idealism, are deadening influences against which even fear may be beneficially effective. I was much impressed when a headmaster once told me that he had heard grown men, who were bringing their sons to school, roundly curse their own schoolmasters who had not punished them— the fathers—into strenuousness. Kipling prefixes to *Stalky & Co.* a poem to which I used to make frequent allusions in assembly and staff meetings, and in which the following words occur in commendation of ' the famous men set in office o'er us ' because they

> Beat on us with rods,
> Faithfully with many rods,
> Daily beat on us with rods,
> For the love they bore us.

Even-handed justice never harms anyone, but is very difficult to administer. It was not because I disapproved of punishment, but because I found the task of fitting the punishment to the culprit and holding the balance beyond my powers that I fell back on something less emphatic and lengthier.

I feel sure that in certain recent discussions there has

been a confusion of thought between *repression* and *restraint*. Repression of instinct is dangerous because man is a beast; restraint is necessary to him because he is *not* a beast. I was once visiting a friend who was the proud possessor of a rather new baby, and was invited to be present at his evening toilet so that I might admire his many perfections. When I saw the nurse unrolling and removing what seemed to me quite unnecessary swathings, I was moved to remark that it seemed a pity to bind up his little trunk—why not leave him free like the jolly little animal he was? The nurse put me wise in a moment. " Excuse me, Miss, that's where you're wrong; he isn't an animal. He's a christian and got such a temper of his own that he would soon scream his insides out of joint if I didn't put his binder on." In theory she was right. We are too spiritual to dispense with restraint. The aim of school discipline is to provide a wise restraint until the process of spiritual development is advanced and the soul assumes control. That is the ideal, and one excellent test of the efficiency of discipline is the tone of the upper school. The Sixth should be free from school discipline, having developed the faculty of self-restraint, or, as we usually call it, self-control.

My heart misgives me as I write. Never was self-control more needed than at the present when the very term is sneered at. How often is a life marred by a single unrestrained impulse! Surely those who speak glibly of dispensing with discipline do not realize what it means to train children to think that the mood of the moment is to be the determining factor of a situation—that what is hard may be shirked and the disagreeable avoided. Reaction from the heavy-handed methods of our ancestors has gone too far. I have formed the opinion that, as a whole, educationists are apt to go to extremes. Educational conferences are numerous and the temptation to go one better than the previous speaker leads to overbalance and fallacy. I once heard a headmistress say that she had only two rules in her school: that the girls should bow their heads at prayers, and have a pocket large enough to accommodate a handkerchief. I have always wondered why she drew the line at prayers and pocket handkerchiefs.

When our only disciplinary procedure was the reporting to the headmistress, I had much experience in getting at the heart of disciplinary difficulties. Practically all offences arose from one cause—dull teaching and faults in class management. When the Snellham girls were interested in their work—and they were of a kind to be rather easily interested—they were ' good '. But one ineffective teacher often upsets the whole apple-cart. I always much disliked these interviews and probably for that very reason—I was a success at them. It is, I suppose, a matter of common experience to find oneself strangely successful at tasks about which one has felt misgivings: the whole spiritual force within is called to the struggle. I never interviewed a girl on any subject of more than ordinary complexity without feeling anxious whether I should say or do the right thing. In time, my methods became almost stereotyped. First of all, I used to warn the girl against self-defence at the expense of truth. I deferred all questioning until I had done this, and if, in haste to justify herself, the culprit began her story before I had time to get in the warning, I used to stop her. *Lying in self-defence is almost instinctive.* Here is the true function of the school: to strengthen the spiritual so that it may not be deposed from its rightful post of supreme power. My girls did not tell lies easily, and many of them suffered when they had done so. I have watched with silent admiration and passionate sympathy, the strugglings of little souls at the testing. I do thank Lord Bacon for having described a lie as being ' brave before God, and cowardly before men '. English girls hate the idea of cowardice, and I never allowed my school to forget that lying and cowardice are inseparables. On the last day of my headmistress-ship, five girls came to confess to misstatements they had made to me, the memory of which hurt their self-respect—that most precious spiritual possession, which all disciplinarians should beware of injuring by deed or word or implication. One after the other they explained they did not want me to go away with a false impression, and four of them said they had been cowards. In reality they were seeking to be reinstated in their own esteem. It is a cardinal error to take a child unawares, as I learnt from the following experience. I was investigating the truth of a report that a certain girl had been behaving rowdily with a boy admirer. On entering the room, the culprit anticipated proceedings by promptly informing me that the boy was her cousin. This took the wind out of my sails and I paused to take my bearings. Suddenly, I saw the girl's saucy little face cloud over and her head droop; she gulped, tried to speak, failed, tried again, and just as I was concluding that she was going to have a fit of some kind, she blurted out, " He wasn't my cousin." I still remained silent, trying to guess at the motive of this bald avowal, and she gasped out, " I won't tell a lie about it." Her courage had risen to the sticking-place. How thankful I was that my momentary pauses had allowed time for the Holy Spirit to work in the young soul and for conscience to climb back to her throne.

Another of my principles was never to introduce religion in my interviews. It is hard for me to sort out my reasons for this course, it was so nearly instinctive. Perhaps a reaction against something in my early training, perhaps personal sensitiveness to the claims of religion; possibly a feeling that I should be using a weapon the effects of which would be, for good or ill, beyond my control; possibly a feeling that it wasn't quite fair in the case of someone unable to escape from what might be too scarifying to be borne. Not that I kept religion in the background, out of sight in my school. On the contrary, it permeated my lessons, shone through my assembly addresses, but in disciplinary interviews it was conspicuous by its absence. Rummaging my memory I think I, very early in my experience, formed the idea that children were very secretly sensitive on such matters, for I can recall one or two passionate outbursts when, innocently and mildly, I inquired of some obstinately naughty child whether she didn't care whether she did right or wrong. Even that simple inquiry seemed to touch the quick in the child heart, and I had no wish to do that. In retrospect, I see it was the only thing I personally could do and that, as a whole, it was wise. There is a tendency among young people to associate religion with prohibitions, and I am glad I did nothing to encourage that way of thinking. My trump card was an appeal to common sense. Snellhamites had a great regard for common sense. I used to weary of the sound of a word which was often used to clinch an argument in favour of the present rather than the future, of the actual rather than the ideal. Common sense has its uses—I acknowledge my indebtedness to it—but I prefer that kind of sense which is less common and which I feel myself unable to define lest it should turn out to be no *sense* at all. My girls had a great deal of common sense, and when I pointed out that lessons must be learnt before examinations can be passed, that parents and local authorities do not pay fees for girls who get bad reports, and that education ' makes all the difference ' in one's future, they usually stopped playing monkey tricks. As a whole they were both spirited and amenable —a rare combination. They were of the type that plays a losing game best, and listens to reason. Also, they found the rules unprovocative and the lessons reasonably interesting. That dull teaching was at the root of most of our disciplinary troubles made things difficult for me, as I have never been persuaded in my own mind that children should be blamed for refusing to be bored. I do not know whether they should be forced to listen to dull teaching without, at least, the protest of fidgets.

I feel that more children are dulled than are born dull, and as long as we teach in masses—wrongly called classes—in our primary schools, so long will the result be disappointing. Teachers cannot do justice to large numbers of children of various types and at different stages of development. Without individual attention it is inevitable that some fall behind, lose interest and are bored into mischief. These are the fortunate ones. Less happy is the child who, in fear of penalty, falls back on himself and, the process of introversion beginning or continuing, grows dull and listless. Thus is stupidity manufactured wholesale. It would make for progress in this very imperfect educational world if every child, as soon as he began to be bored, were to emit automatically a squeak—such as some dolls make when squeezed in their middles. The local authorities would soon find funds to stop the row and scores of teachers make a hurried exit from the profession, their fingers in their ears.

The habit of inattention is formed when children are forced to listen to what they cannot understand, without opportunity to ask what it all means. Teachers have to counter this habit and for that reason only clever teachers succeed with dullards. It is thought-provoking to watch children, as I have so often done, at a lecture or during an address. For a few minutes they take stock of the speaker and, if he or she is peculiar in any way, the attention is detained for some few minutes. Later, with the younger ones, they try hard to sit still and, if the headmistress is there, do so. But it's not good for them. Some children settle down at once to inattention. This is because, in their experience, the speaker is almost sure to be hard to follow, and they soon give up all hope of getting anything out of the proceedings. If the boys and girls of schools are what visitors describe as ' easy to talk to ', it may be safely assumed that the talkers (teachers) of that school are not, as a whole, uninteresting. The children do not expect to be bored.

The last of the chief characteristics of my interviewing was perhaps the most useful in its effects. I never closed an interview on any serious matter without saying something to pave the way for, or, at least, to suggest, that great moral process which we lightly describe as *turning over a new leaf.* Common sense again. " If you tumble down in the mud, you do not stay there. You scramble to your feet as quickly as you can, set bravely to work to get the dirt off, and take good care not to be so careless as to fall down again." In how many hundreds of cases have I seen the light of resolution replace the sullenness of conscious wrong-doing, and the slouch give way to a poise of self-respect! It is most important that a girl should be on good terms with *herself* before she leaves the headmistress. She should also have a picture of herself in the future as respected by others. A girl in disgrace is a very unsatisfactory case. All moral progress is made in the ebb and flow way, not only the progress of the *individual* but of the race itself. It was part of my system to suggest the making of a fresh start whenever times and seasons made such suggestion opportune. At such times I felt that good resolutions were in the very air: I sensed them in the poise of the little tunic-clad figures and in the spick-and-span-ness of the whole aspect. I used to listen to the girls—who in turns, by forms, chose the hymns for prayers — singing with cheerful gusto Clough's verses beginning " Say not the struggle naught availeth ", and hope passionately that no one of them might ever be a prey to spiritual despair.

The normal girl does not enjoy wrong-doing. If she appears to do so, there is something wrong in the way of things. (Outburst of high spirits during a dull lesson is not wrong-doing.) I was very severe on anything that hindered the work of the class, and allowed no excuses to avail against penalties for disturbance of the teaching. Such disturbance rarely happens with efficient teachers *throughout* a school, but poor discipline in only one or two classes affects the whole, and weighs heavily on the rest of the staff. I formed the opinion that such offences were often due to impulse and best treated by the girls themselves on the spot. I therefore arranged for the election by the girls of each form of a captain, vice-captain and committee, who would be always at hand to remind the thoughtless and check the wilful. Mutual help fostered by a form spirit in favour of good work resulted. The form mistress who acted as adviser to the committee was relieved of the duty of correcting little points of speech and behaviour as the captains saw to everything that brought discredit on the form. Again I express admiration of some of the form mistresses who worked out this system with me, especially of the knack they acquired of influencing without interfering; of

suggesting by using some such tentative expressions as,
" I wonder whether . . ." or, " Have you ever thought
of . . . ?" In form management the word *don't* should
be almost superfluous, for prevention is better than cure.
But this kind goeth not forth but by prayer and fasting,
and who is sufficient for these things?

A headmistress who is backed by a complete set of
clever and devoted form mistresses is omnipotent, and
no further development would have been necessary had
that happy experience been mine. As it was, little difficulties kept recurring and I decided to call in prefect
help. At first, a prefect was assigned to each form, and
I still dealt with the reported cases. Later, I saw the
wisdom of giving greater responsibility to the prefects
and, in the event, passed the reported cases to certain of
them who were known as ' prefects of the court '.

My decision to take this step, which seemed at the
time almost revolutionary, was influenced by the discovery of the beneficial effect of responsibility on the
girls in the upper school. The result was one of the
triumphs of my professional life. The shouldering of the
burden of responsibility makes for happiness in as much
as it satisfies the instinct for power. Girls above the age
of sixteen or seventeen are ripe for rule of some kind,
and delight in rising to the occasion. I handed it over
very completely because I disbelieve in what is called
divided responsibility. Ultimately a complete system was
established, something as follows: All sixth form girls
were prefects, but the nature of the responsibility assigned to them varied considerably. Certain of the second

year were made ' prefects of the court ' and held a weekly
tribunal which dealt with the week's reported cases. The
Senior Prefect presided at the court and the smooth
working of the whole system depended on her. Only
once did my Senior fail me; most of them managed
to remain popular in spite of their disciplinary function.
One thing I learnt—to avoid choosing girls who in-
herited the tendency to scold, and the parentage and home
environment of the senior prefect became a factor to be
considered in the selection. The court assembled round
the platform table at the end of our large hall, and the
culprits with their form captains, out of earshot at the
other end, awaited a summons to it. The procedure was
as follows. First the Senior asked both captain and culprit to speak freely about the circumstances which led to
the reporting. Next—in order to make sure that a mere
lapse of tongue or memory was not being treated as an
offence—the Senior was bound, by a very strict rule, to
ask the culprit whether she had been *personally* warned
that repetition of, or persistence in, the offence would
lead to a report to the court. If the reply was in the
negative—if the warning had been general—to the *form*
and not to the *individual*—then the court had no jurisdiction. Otherwise the court either at once, or later
after deliberation, imposed a penalty, which was generally
of the nature of detention or the imposition of some
little task of memorizing—all of which the prefects
arranged for and supervised. With girls the sting of
punishment lies, not in the penalty but in the disgrace.
As soon as the court rose, the senior prefect came to my

room—I was always at hand—and reported the proceedings. I rarely had much to revise: to point out that the task of learning the selected piece of French poetry was beyond the range of the culprit's form, or that so-and-so was not very well and must be let off easily and so forth. The commonplaces of practical discipline—that girls often appear defiant when they are secretly only angry with themselves; that publicity in punishment hurts the self-respect and must be avoided like poison; that punishment is not *in itself* a deterrent but rather, at any rate with school girls, a poignant reminder that things are not as they should be and so forth—had all been thrashed out before the responsibility was entrusted to the court. The girls were restrained and wise far beyond their years, and, in retrospect, I marvel at their discretion.

As I have already said the most common offence which came before the court was inattention in class, leading to disturbance of the teaching. The penalty for this was fixed—a ' report card '. This card had on it certain spaces for the initials of the mistresses who taught the holder of the card, seven spaces per day, thirty-five in all. At the end of afternoon school, this card had to be brought to me for my signature, and no card was withdrawn until it recorded that all the spaces had been duly initialled, as a sign that satisfaction had been given throughout a whole week. This arrangement gave me my chance: I had a personal interview daily for a week with every girl who was the cause of interruption in class time, and a firm hold on that most important part of school discipline. My usual appeals to common sense proved very effective, few girls having a second report card and only one, during the whole decade of this prefect control, incurring the disgrace of a third. I use the word *disgrace* advisedly, for I managed to make the girls feel the odium of so much supervision. " Do you like being tied to my apron strings like this?" I would inquire scornfully. Great is the effect of terse description. Apron-stringing became abhorrent to all self-respecting girls. The average number of cases reported to the Prefects' Court per week was about three, not including the one or two occasions when whole forms were *summoned*—rather than reported. Minutes were carefully kept and, when I left, there were records available giving details of names, punishments, offences for the whole decade of prefect jurisdiction.

The advantages of this system over all others I have heard of or tried are as follows: first, it gave opportunity for public, or form, spirit to play its part; second, it made the girls more individually responsible for the reputation of their form and ultimately of their school; third, the girls were not exposed to the temptation of self-defence at the expense of truth, each case having already been investigated by the form committee; fourth, it was possible to get a much clearer idea of what was going on in the school, because the girls spoke freely to the prefects and did not feel they were ' peaching ' on anyone. It also abolished that most odious possibility of pouncing on girls unawares, catching them ' at it '. My soul used to rise up against that sort of thing. I hate to hear girls scuffling and scurrying at the approach of authority, and I plead guilty to advertising my approach, if only by a cough, when I thought I was coming on girls unawares.

The disadvantages were as follows: the girls disliked going before the court almost too intensely. Hence the few cases reported. I know that punishment must not be pleasurable and that the adolescent is capable of extracting pleasure—that is notoriety—out of the most unpleasant things. But there is a limit in that direction. Second, there was sometimes a charge brought that certain prefects were prejudiced against certain girls or forms. I never found the slightest evidence that it was so, but, as I am informed such charges are brought against all schools, even against those strongholds of prefect rule, the Public Schools, I refer to it as a possibility. I am glad to remember that, although the public school tradition was practically unknown in Snellham, there were signs that the parents were coming to realize that there was a lack of good taste in cavilling at the findings of prefects, and much wisdom in leaving their children to face the rough and tumble of school life on their own. It was the over-parented and the spoilt child with an inordinate opinion of its importance who found the court too impersonal, and went home with exaggerated tales of its horrors.

The practical difficulty about this system is the keeping everyone up to the mark. Mistresses who have been reared on ' order marks ', as I was myself, may not be able to shake off the shackles of old systems, and prefer popping on girls at odd time with marks and detentions and so forth. For success, the system requires a capable and public-spirited Sixth, a staff not too conservative or too elderly to make use of the unfamiliar, live wires as form mistresses and a headmistress with a concealed knack of turning up exactly when and where she is wanted, and of lying low when she isn't.

The school changed with its system of discipline: it is hard to express exactly in what the difference consisted, but it was a distinct change. Perhaps it will suffice if I say that, as I stood at the door of my room and watched the forms filing past, I became aware of a gradual change in the expressions on their faces. Formerly, it had been vaguely interrogative. Now it was reassuring, as who should say: " Quite all right, Miss Cleeve, we're looking after things." Each girl, consciously or otherwise, grew more responsible in her attitude towards the school. Especially was this noticeable in the upper school. The Sixth form rose to its responsibilities finely: they ceased to be a source of anxiety and before they left we found them already most companionable, and delightfully appreciative. The formation of a vigorous Old Girls Association followed as a matter of course.

When I realized the effect of responsibility on the older girls, I rummaged my brain and exhausted my resources to create little spheres for little people and to use such spheres and all other little posts of responsibility as safety valves for girls conscious of growing powers. Not infrequently, I passed over the chairmanship of a school meeting to a girl or to a member of staff, betaking myself to the back of the hall and making myself useful as a good clapper of the speaker's points.

I enjoyed seeing my nurslings play at grown-ups: there was much humour in the situation. The kindergarten and preparatory staff at that time were keen on the same sort of thing, so that, in addition to all manner of clubs in the main school—dramatic, lecture, poetry, science, as well as games—the preparatory spread itself out in the same direction. I remember a concert given by the babies over which a chairman named Charlie presided. He was so self-important that he aspirated wherever it was humanly possible. " The next *h*item is Billy," he announced, and Billy came promptly forward and attempted to recite ' Ten little Nigger Boys ', collapsing at the end of each line that presented arithmetical difficulties and being somewhat scornfully helped out by his audience. Then ' Doris ' came forward as the ' next *h*item ' and danced a few steps as much with her wriggling shoulders as with her feet. (The fact that I remember so clearly proves what the psychologists tell us —that pleasurable emotion stimulates and deepens perception.)

As most of my prefects were preparing for examination, I had to be very careful not to overwork them. I found it useful to have the whole Sixth as prefects, because they could be called upon at a minute's notice to do deputy work for the staff, and they kept themselves organized for sudden calls of the kind. I had only to intimate that I wished to speak to the staff at the close of the morning assembly to ensure that, at the proper moment, each prefect would march straight to her post of duty, and, if a staff meeting was held at the close of school, with the same promptitude and perfect efficiency, they undertook to dismiss the forms and take the cloak-room duty. Their power of self-organization varied very little from year to year; as a rule they showed themselves as competent as the staff. This competency was, in fact, due to association with mistresses who were clever organisers, from whom they learnt the trick of prompti-tude and effectiveness. They were naturally impatient of muddling and fuss.

Twice during the war, to compensate for the length of time spent on railway travelling, I gave my staff an extra day's leave. At the end of afternoon school, I told the prefects that I should depend on them for the teaching and management of the school on the morrow, giving them some general directions. Without more ado they set to work to rearrange the timetable and assign duties, the first girl in the Literary Sixth assum-ing the responsibility of the work of the Senior English specialist and so on. The secret was so well kept that a ripple of astonishment passed over the whole school at prayers next morning when the prefects lined up in the places usually occupied by the staff. I arranged that each teaching period should be shortened from forty-five to forty minutes. Otherwise everything went on as usual, the decorum being, if anything, excessive. Nothing was forgotten, not even the carving at dinner. Throughout the day, with the exception of the kitchen staff, I was the only adult in the building. I never had a quieter day. When I presented myself at the door of Form III to give the scheduled scripture lesson, I was informed that the prefects, being under the impression that I should be too busy to teach, had arranged a games period as an option.   I withdrew, thinking furiously. At the close of afternoon school, as the senior prefect was hanging up the keys in my room, she remarked that she thought responsibility was ' a little wearing '. I agreed with her: responsibility *is* ' a little wearing '.

CHAPTER VI

Disciplinary Influences

The chief disciplinary influence in a school—the influence which is felt by all who are connected with it and which permeates every department of its working—is usually called *tone*. Tone is aptly so called because it suggests melody. Every school has its own melody, which should not be only pleasing but well-marked and easily distinguishable no matter through how many contrapuntal labyrinths and variations it may run. It is well if it be of such a haunting nature as to persist through the noise and bustle of adult life and be easily convertible into a bugle call to duty. By all means it must have a lilt about it. I believe in lilt as a great moral force. I like to get a glimpse of it in the streets and architecture of a town—Snellham streets had no lilt at all. I rejoice when I hear it tinkling out in laughter and note its effect on the trimming of hats. I adore it in the crocus and daffodil which come in spring to set the world a-lilting. It is incarnate in the thrush and made St. Francis a '*jongleur de Dieu*'. I look for it in hymns and am thankful for it in sermons—when I can get it. Sometimes I catch at it in prayers, where it depends upon the soul of the clergyman. I remember once hearing it ring out so clearly in the petition, " May it please Thee to strengthen such as do stand, to comfort and help the weakhearted, to raise up them that fall, and FINALLY to beat down Satan under our feet ", that I wonder the congregation did not jump at the sound of the word *finally*. It sounded for all the world like a *pas seul de joie* or a distant pæan of victory, and must have reached the souls of the falling and the weakhearted. When one comes to think of it, prayers ought to be full of lilt. Christ's teaching is instinct with it, and the world is still agape at the magnificent *insouciance* of such sayings as, " Let the morrow take care of the things of itself " and " If a man smite thee on the one cheek, turn to him the other also ". Lilt is essential to the working of a successful school. It must sound out in the Head's " Good Morning " as she appears on the platform, and resound in the hymns and prayers; it should echo in every class room and a sorry thing indeed is a lesson without it. But—who is sufficient for these things? Blessed is the headmistress who, like Benedick's Beatrice, was born when ' there was a star danced ', and woe to those clumsy officials and administrators who by heavy handling crush the song out of the throat of the singing bird.

The atmosphere of the school should be favourable to culture and the pupils alive to the charm of knowledge. What the headmistress and staff love and admire will ultimately affect the likes and dislikes of the school. But enthusiasm, thank God, is catching, and one flickering torch may kindle many fires. The glow is the thing.

Books recommended or lent, travels described, talks about the beauty of poem or picture, expressions of admiration for great writers of the present day, with specific allusions to fine passages in their works, bits of information about great undertakings—Egyptian excavations, Polar expeditions, the *Oxford English Dictionary*—all are propaganda in favour of culture. The Head's influence is, of course, conditioned by her popularity but is likely to be greater than the rest put together. The headmistress who gave her senior pupils ' a gala afternoon ' on the day some thirty years ago when the copyright ran out, and the first collected edition of Browning's poems was purchasable at a reasonable price, was on the right track in so far as she was emphasizing what was truly an event in the world of culture.

It was an up-to-(present)-date psychologist who nearly two thousand years ago advised his correspondents to ' overcome evil with good '. The taste for cheap finery, unworthy amusements, meretricious art and sensational fiction can be countered only by substituting the *love* of the best. " Do you not feel discouraged," asked a vicar of Snellham, " when, after all your pains to recommend the tasteful and refined, your girls, on leaving, revert to their former tawdriness in dress?" " I'm afraid I didn't look nice enough," was my dolefully truthful reply. Again, who is sufficient for these things? If, however, we are unable, by reason of human frailty, always to recommend the true, the good, and the beautiful, we may refrain from hindering the progress of such agencies as make for what is lovely and of good report, and it is wise to make a rule never to criticize what tends to edification in the hearing of those who *in any way* are weaker than ourselves. I found that certain members of my staff needed cautioning in this matter. I marvel at the amount of weak scepticism which results from a university course and finds its way into a staff room. There is one condemnation—the sternest ever uttered by Our Lord—which we teachers do well to heed. It was pronounced against the man who puts a stumbling-block in the way of ' one of these little ones '. " It is better," said the gentle Jesus, " that a millstone were hanged about his neck and that he were cast into the sea."

The creation in our schools of this atmosphere favourable to culture is the more difficult because the national trend is not in that direction. In a subtle but very real way, stupidity and a certain kind of ignorance are more than tolerated in England. Compared with the studious boy, the dunce has the popular honours. Even in such papers as *Punch*, a premium is set upon the barbarian type of boy, in that the studious youth is often depicted as absurdly solemn, spectacled and knock-kneed. Howlers, presumably, are so called because they make people howl with laughter; they are, nevertheless, the signs of muddle-headedness and ineptitude. Speech days have often a like effect. With that fatal tendency to the auto-biographical which is characteristic of local orators, the chairman of the governing body, in his introductory remarks, owns to having left school at a very early age or without scholastic honours, the audience being implicitly invited to admire him for having climbed to his present dazzling municipal eminence without the aid of education. After that, his peroration on the superior advantages of boys at the present day falls flat. " Self-made men ought to be muzzled at prize-givings," whispered a university committee representative, " they are such awful bores." " They are worse than bores," I replied. " There is nothing worse," he persisted. It was something worse than boredom that made me feel sick at heart: it was the total lack of inspiration. No one seemed in the least conscious of the charm of knowledge for its own fair sake. If the distinguished visitor happened to be a university professor, things were not quite at their worst, and the bored appearance of many of these erudite gentlemen may have been a disguise. It had, however, a depressing effect especially when combined with that inaudibility of speech which is so often the result of lecturing to students who do not take lectures very seriously. But when a moneyed or titled Philistine distributed the prizes, he invariably confessed to an inglorious school career and, after sympathizing lengthily with those of his audience who had won no prizes, he passed on to congratulations on the games records and expressions of his behalf in the ' educational value of athletics ' (why are so many sermons addressed to the converted?), and sat down without referring to the value of knowledge, unless, perchance, it had led to scholarship successes. His genial appearance (' a jolly old boy '), the rumours of his wealth, and the appearance of his Rolls Royce at the school entrance did the trick: the boys agreed with him that boys will be boys, and went on being boys with all their might and main. If only such occasions could be used to bring the youth of our schools into contact with truly great men and women—those who have realized some of their ideals and ambitions; if, as might happen with really large-souled men and women, they told them simply, without official palaver, of their path of progress; when enthusiasm first possessed them; what schools and colleges they attended, what honours they had gained; in what consisted their respective contributions to the sum of the world's knowledge and added personal touches such as would have the effect of making the whole seem *livable*, a torch would be lighted in England that would never be extinguished. For youth is bursting with suppressed idealism. There are few stupid children in our schools, but thousands who are not roused to make the best of themselves. Young Snellham was quickly responsive, naturally earnest and intelligent.

The real love of knowledge seems to be rarer than ever. Tennyson asked what I believe he meant to be a rhetorical question. " Who loves not knowledge? Who shall rail against her beauty?" No one actually *rails*—unless the use of the term *stuffy* may be dignified as railing—but the majority of English youth are indifferent and many openly contemptuous. Epithets such as *highbrow*, *early victorian*, *a back number* avail to nip enthusiasms in the bud. I have lived to hear Shakespeare called a ' back number ', and Browning described as ' stuffy '. There is in some circles a shyness about owning to a fondness for intellectual pursuits. In 1912, I was staying at a hotel with a party which included two German girls who were finishing their education by a year's study of English Literature in England. At dinner the aberrations of unskilled waiters amused us, and one of the party, as he was stretching out to reach an errant sauceboat, remarked, " A man's reach should exceed his grasp." A discussion followed as to which of Browning's poems the line belonged. As I had brought my volumes of Browning with me, I remarked that the question could be settled when dinner was over. One of the Germans, declaring she couldn't eat any more till she knew, asked permission to fetch the book, and presently returned with it open, announcing proudly that ' we Germans have backed the right horse '. The scene attracted the attention of other diners, one of whom, in virtue of his special knowledge of Germany and Germans, described the episode as ' characteristically German '. It was certainly not characteristically English. Few schoolgirls, and fewer schoolboys, would have recognized the quotation, and I cannot imagine many English people leaving the business of *table d'hôte* to verify his or her opinion on a subject of such abstract importance. We limit strictly the number of things about which *good form*—that " last and basest of man's many servitudes " (as someone has called it)—permits the open expression of enthusiasm, and the greatest of these is athletics. (Another, so I understand from contemporary fiction, is *dogs*, and a third the culture—I use a euphemistic word—of pigs.)

I had many opportunities for ascertaining the views of the Snellhamites as to the advantages of what they called

' a good education ', and I found their expressions of opinion thought-provoking. " Jessie is getting on well," said a mother, " she doesn't laugh at the same things as she used to." It was a father who said that he had noticed that educated people had a different look on their faces, adding, " I should like my girl's face to look like that." I once overheard a conversation between a headmaster and an irate father who had come to complain that his son was devoting too much time to sport. The headmaster defended his *régime* by asking, " Isn't it enough if I turn out capable, clean-living boys?" " By God, it isn't," was the forcible rejoinder, " I want my boy to use his brains and have something in his head to steady him." The three parents were on the right track. The father had my sympathy. It is not within my range to pronounce on the educational value of games in a boys' school—I appreciate their value in a girls' school— but am conscious that there is a danger of forgetting that the mind is the predominant partner in the human combine and that something to think about, as well as to catch and kick, is needed for a healthy mind in a healthy body. For, in most cases, evil thought precedes evil action, and the ancient code which said ' Thou shalt not covet ' as well as ' Thou shalt not steal ' was in reality duplicating the prohibition of a common offence as well as conforming to the findings of modern psychology.

I know exactly what Marion's father meant when he alluded to a changed facial expression as one of the desirable effects of education. And now—we touch upon the innermost secret joy of a headmistress's life. To watch the roving, shifty eyes grow steadfast, the carriage of the head more self-respecting, to trace in gentler manners the springing of courtesy in the soul, and in a more fearless demeanour the dawn of conscious rectitude —these are the triumphs over which a headmistress rejoices in secret with a joy unspeakable and thanksgivings manifold. Compared with this, what matter if governors grump and gruntle, forget to be gracious and choose deliberately to be unjust? *We have our day*.

The opinion expressed by Jessie's mother I found exceedingly interesting. Nothing betrays character and breeding more clearly than laughter, which, at best, is delightful, at its worst, devilish. People differ so widely as to what they think funny. Some detect humour in a man chasing his hat in a wind; others are convulsed at an allusion to a maiden aunt. I have met those who find no fun in Dickens, and I myself am but faintly interested in Charlie Chaplin's feet. I remember giving leave of absence to a little Jewish boy because, as his father wrote, " next week is a festival of our holy religion, and I wish my son to take part." On the boy's return from these religious solemnities, he set the whole Preparatory a-laughing at his imitation of " Charlie ". Children's laughter is sweet, and I would fain have it evoked by what is uplifting as well as funny. I recognize in laughter something that is natural to healthy young life. I have come across hundreds of school boys and girls travelling to and from schools, all reading comic papers—colloquially known as ' comics '—to wile away the time and have a good laugh. Girls often did worse in buying sentimental story papers, about beauteous beings whose course of true love never did run smooth till the last page or two, when they either got married or died and let worms eat them—for love, of course. I once caught sight of a sentimental scrap of a girl wiping away a furtive tear as she perused one of these twopenny numbers. I asked for the loan of it, which she granted after warning me that it was ' very sad '. I was relieved to find that, although the heroine's shingle and her skill in the latest dance were minutely described, it was satisfactorily victorian in its restraint. But I was jealous of the emotion roused by such silly stuff: I knew how potent in the youthful mind wholesome emotion can be, and I longed to harness it to great causes. One day I was deputizing for an absent mistress and used the period for reading aloud from *David Copperfield*—the account of his first day at school, the pathos of his loneliness, and the cruelty of the placard on his back, *Take care of him he bites*. A muffled sound made me look up and see a little red-haired child leaning her head against the dado in an effort to control her sobs. As I ceased reading, she burst out into sobs and invective against the perpetrators of the injustice. The whole class joined in and, for a few seconds, we were an indignation meeting protesting against all the injustice and cruelty meted out to children since the beginning of time. That outburst I call *wholesome* emotion, being sure that a quickening of sympathy with the victims of tyranny and injustice would result. An elementary schoolmaster once complained to me that my girls had disturbed the peace of the railway carriage in which he and they were travelling Snellham-wards. I asked what they were excited about and he said it was usually some disputed point in their mathematical home-work. I thanked God audibly—much to my interlocutor's astonishment—and took courage inaudibly. It was better than I had dared to hope.

Environment, as we all know, plays an important part in character development. My work was the easier because the school building had a certain dignity about it which attracted, but did not overpower, the young mind. It would have been a mistake for Snellham to have a school building of a heavily academic type, and a greater mistake to have one of a mean appearance. The growing power of appreciation in the child mind may be impaired by prolonged inability to apprehend a beauty of which more developed minds are easily aware. On the other had, facile self-complacency is fostered by constant association with the commonplace. The pictures in a school greatly influence its tone and, for the reason I have just adduced, should be carefully chosen and graded. A good picture always commands attention, but is not always appreciated—seeing they see but do not perceive. It is easy to cast pearls where they may not be trampled on but where they lie neglected. The upper school should have only masterpieces on its walls, but prejudice against the finest pictures may be created if they are not explained to the younger children. I do not agree that a child should be left to find out artistic excellence for himself: much time may be wasted, or he may never do so. I remember telling a group of girls

that, when I had found myself unable to keep up with
friends walking along the seashore, I had sat down to
watch the shadows on the sea. " Are there shadows on
the sea?" asked one whose faculty of observation had
evidently escaped training. She might easily have missed,
even for life, the joy of cloud shadows. However much
one may long to be alone in the presence of beauty, it
would be grossly selfish to steal away to gaze alone on the
alpengluh and never to tell one's fellow diners at *table
d'hôte* that heaven is touching earth on the snowy heights.

My school was spacious and its corridors wide, and for
this I was unfeignedly thankful. For jostling develops
into pushing and encourages bad manners generally.
When girls are huddled together, personality is not so
easily recognized nor individuality fostered. There was
educational value in the orderly filing along the corridors:
the girls enjoyed it, the form captains taking pride in the
arrangement of the files. The mere walking across the
vacant floor space of a large hall tends to lessen self-
consciousness and develop a feeling of independence.
I encouraged this orderly filing even in the kindergarten.
Children love anything that has a touch of the processional
about it: it satisfies both self and herd instincts and makes
them feel like grown-ups. The current delusion that
children are happy only when free from control had its
origin in the revolt from the rigidity of the last generation.

I made great use of the school assembly short addresses,
which, in spite of the fact that I never thought them out
beforehand, seem to have been amazingly effective. I
have received scores of testimonies to their helpfulness,

from old girls and parents, and attribute this success to the intensity of my purpose in delivering them. I was a very anxious headmistress, watchful of tendencies, apprehensive of wrong developments, and I believed that prevention was better than cure. Only when I thought that danger threatened, did the spirit move me to speak. In retrospect, I see myself too forcible, as nervous people often are, and I detect two main currents in my exhortations—one which aimed at encouraging, and another which aimed at winning allegiance to whatever I thought admirable. Generations of girls—a scholastic generation extends over five or six years—have filed out of the hall with the clang of Rudyard Kipling's words sounding in their ears:

> Man must finish off his work,
> Right or wrong, his daily work,
> And without excuses;

for I am a strong believer in the desirability of the strenuous life and naturally scornful of slackness and shuffling. Some of my ' old girls ' have ventured to tease me about the frequency with which, during the dark days of winter (when getting up in the mornings is *so* hard for little sleepy-heads), I used to fire off a question which was really a loose translation from Marcus Aurelius: " Is a man good for nothing but to lie under a counter-pane?" I learnt to be cautious in my use of praise. Timely praise is useful as it inspires to further effort; facile praise is futile and recoils on the utterer. " Does the Head really think this is my best work?" asked a keen-

witted girl scornfully. " Why, I did it on my knee in the
train coming to school this morning!"   " She praises
everything," commented her companion.   " Then she
praises nothing," was the apt rejoinder of the keen-witted
and scornful one.   I believe it is wise to praise *effort*
rather than achievement, and with young children there
is not much risk in so doing.   But undeserved praise
tends to check effort, and in dealing with the undeveloped
that is a most undesirable result.   The road *does* wind
uphill all the way, and moral muscle must not be allowed
to become flaccid.   Moreover, it is wise to let virtue be its
own reward sometimes: the habit of expecting to be
praised for doing that which is our duty to do is a dangerous one.   Ridicule is also a weapon I was afraid of
using, its effect on so many different temperaments is
incalculable.   Caricature of a mildly humorous kind
avails in the tackling of such failings as affectation and
swelled-headed-ness, but it must be strictly impersonal.
Thank God for Dickens and the sweetness of his humour.

The other aim of my addresses was to make the girls
admire what is admirable.   This was a pleasant task, for
girls naturally love the lovely.   As I have said elsewhere,
they were gritty rather than gracious, and I remember
how I spent myself in praise of ' that beautiful thing called
graciousness '.   Personally I would rather be called
gracious than clever, or brilliant or charming or sweet or
all of these put together.   I love to think of the gracious
women I have known.   There was an *aura* about them—
a subtly sweet emanation from the soul.   Their touch was
gentle, their presence, a joy; nervousness and its atten-

dant awkwardness vanished under their influence. It were impossible to imagine them turning the cold shoulder or administering a snub, for is not graciousness a blend of the highest human breeding with a touch of the divine charity? The beauty of such traits of character is best taught by reference to the lives of the Saints and to the life of Our Lord. The prayer that ' the grace of Our Lord Jesus be ever with us ' will then gain additional meaning. The moment when a girl first realizes the reality of *moral* beauty marks the beginning of another phase in soul development.

I am conscious that a great change is coming over the ideals of the rising generation. With the best will in the world, I am not able to admire the ' modern girl '. I do not believe she is more fearless and straightforward than we were. I have known her *slavish* in her fear of being out of the swim, and is not the motive of her paint and powder to mislead? I see in her vaunted independence only the satisfaction of self-instinct. I ascribe her scorn of tradition to self-conceit. Her flippancy bores me; her slangy speech sets my teeth on edge, and the sound of her incessant laughter sends me to bed where I dive under the bedclothes to escape it.

The advantage of mooring one's bark in a backwater is that it escapes the backwash from larger craft on the main stream. Thus was it with me in Snellham, none of these things disturbed me. It is different now, and I am thankful to have escaped before my boat began to oscillate. For a headmistress must never wobble or be uncertain in what way she should steer. She must know, for instance, where to draw the line between prudery and modesty, and between modesty and immodesty, and be thoroughly conversant with the ethics of the rouge pot. The headmistress who hesitates is useless: the errant sheep look up and are not led. No evasion is possible for the faithful, and the necessity for readjustment presses. Perhaps Tennyson's words are apposite:

> Meet is it changes should control
> Our being, lest we rust in ease.
> We all are changed by slow degrees,
> All *but the basis of the soul.*

CHAPTER VII

The Curriculum: Religious Instruction

I am now about to describe what use I made of that one weekly period which has a place on the timetables of most municipal schools and is allotted to what is variously described as Scripture, Divinity, Religious Knowledge, or Religious Instruction. I am undecided what term to use for it in this chapter, and have been trying to recall the name given to it on those Board of Education schedules, from a plethora of which we suffered so inopportunely at the beginning of the school year. But my Innisfree is thousand upon thousands of miles away from Whitehall—had it not been, I should not have fled thither—and memory fails. Perhaps my subconscious may oblige later by bringing up from its awful depths a picture of that Time Analysis sheet, the columns of which always seemed so reluctant to square with statistics elsewhere, in which case I shall adopt the name thereon as the heading of this chapter—a proceeding which, now I come to think about it, reveals a respect for the Board which surprises me.

Left unaided by such associations, I shall decide on the term *Religious Instruction*. I like the associations of the literal meaning of that word *instruction*. When one has a vast field to explore and little time in which to do so, it is not possible to effect anything elaborate. My work was mainly preparation, the laying of a well-arranged foundation, in the hope that the future would provide, either by voluntary study or further teaching, the means of completing the structure. Children listen uncomprehendingly to much religious teaching and I tried to make the understanding of this easier. Moreover, religious instruction is a wide term and extends beyond the ' Scripture period '. All subjects have a theistic background when taught by those who believe—believe *à fond*—in God. Such a history or literature specialist will not miss his opportunity by dawdling over non-essentials, or the art teacher lose himself in technique; the scientist will rejoice at being assigned to a vantage point, and the mathematician not fail to recall that one of the great thinkers of the ancient world adduced mathematical truth as a sign that the gods send messages to men.

The power to apprehend the spiritual in life—so I incline to believe—varies widely in individuals. I, for instance, for a long time, seemed quite unable to form a conception of what was meant by *absolute* beauty, truth, goodness. I am ashamed to own to such crassness, but unable to resist the humiliating conviction that I am not a born ' ghost ' in the sense that ' only ghosts can see ghosts '. (I thank the author of the *Smokeover Legends* for teaching me that epigram.)

It was an uneasy feeling of this kind that led me to regard the apprehension of the spiritual as the aim of religious instruction. On the last day of my headship, when the burden was about to slip from my tired shoulders, a kind of impatience seized me: I wanted to cut short the process of farewells and be free. Especially did I feel disinclined to speak at length in the assembly. When making arrangements for the closing day of the term, I explained this to my staff, some of whom remonstrated, reminding me of the special force which last words are said to possess. As I was girding up myself for the last effort and walking along the corridor to the assembly hall, I tried to decide what was the most important truth I had tried to impress upon the thousands of girls who had attended my Scripture classes and listened to my addresses. In the event, I spoke something as follows: " Of all that I have tried to teach you, there is one truth which I consider most important, and which I want you always to bear in mind—that, behind and above this material world, there is another which, although we cannot apprehend it by our senses, is nevertheless more real, more lasting and vastly more important. Do not lose sight of the spiritual side of life."

The reality of the spiritual is the first great message of the Bible; there are few stories in the Old Testament which may not be used to illustrate this truth and, of course, it is the very stuff and substance of the New. I regard the Bible as the handbook of the Spiritual, a guide to the Invisible, and the textbook of Religious Instruction. It may be possible to gain a knowledge of God without the Bible, but to neglect to avail oneself of its assistance is about as foolish as to attempt to study

history only by observation, without reference to historical
records.   The new-born child, I take it, is nothing but
an animal, and it is the part of true education to assist in
his spiritual development.   As far as my experience goes,
youth aspires.   A fitting symbol of youth would be the
nude, lithe figure of a youth, ' the muscles all a-ripple
on his back ' as he turns towards the heavens, face up-
lifted, hand outstretched.   God does not leave Himself
without a witness in the hearts of the young, and when
the struggle begins

> God stoops o'er his head,
> Satan looks up between his feet—both tug—
> He 's left himself i' the middle: the soul wakes
> And grows.

That is when the school should stand by.

   The Bible needs saving from its friends—those who
read it indistinctly in church, and those who teach it
unintelligently.   Boys and girls are prejudiced against the
Bible when they come to school: they expect to be bored
by it.   It is easy to account for the lack of interest in the
Bible in spite of the fact that it is inherently intensely
interesting: its short stories are the best in all literature,
its poetry among the finest, and its message commends
itself to the minds and consciences of mankind.   It was
only when I came to teach the Bible systematically that
I realized how difficult it is—how much it needs editing.
I think something might be done to make easier the
finding of book, chapter, verse, to reduce the size of the
volume little hands have to hold, and remove the han-

dicap of small type. The Bible might be published in sections with omissions here and there, but with its continuity preserved. With only one weekly period of the nominal length of forty-five minutes, I resented the time spent in turning over pages and reading laboriously from small type. I dared not object to the Bibles brought by the children lest worse should befall. If the Bible were handier it would be read more intelligently. I did not find *complete* ignorance of the Bible wide-spread in that section of the population of Snellham with which I came in contact. But that thousands of school children have little or no idea of it, is a commonplace of experience. Perhaps the time will come when the Christian church will take upon itself the task of seeing to it that every child of school age has provided for it, in its home, a small volume containing the life of Our Lord in the words of the Gospels, with some record from the Acts of the beginnings of the Christian church and some of the plainest of the Apostolic injunctions for christian living. There are enough Bibles to go round, but they are not in circulation. When I was packing to come to my Innisfree, I found I was the possessor of Bibles as follows: one without references, two with ditto, a New Testament and a dainty volume of the Psalms—all of the authorized version; of the revised version, I found one Bible with references, a New Testament; of both versions combined (and interlinear), one Bible which I always used at school. Of other versions, I found myself to possess Bibles in French and German, Moffatt's translation of both testaments, *The New Testament in*

Modern Speech, also a little book of the collected sayings of Christ complied by Professor Mackail, and a Greek Testament. I wondered whether a John the Baptist of the twentieth century would make reply to the effect that ' he that hath two Bibles (to say nothing of expensively bound prayer books), let him give to him that hath none.'

When I have attended conferences on Bible teaching, I have been astonished at the number of teachers who, with only one weekly period, seemed to find time for lessons on subjects which impinge on the Bible record at some point, but are not necessary for an intelligent study of it. I have heard more enthusiastic descriptions of lessons on the code of Amurabbi, the ancient civilizations of the Bible period, excavations, the boyhood of St. Paul, than on the contents of the Bible itself. I have seen examination papers requiring a knowledge of the plagues of Egypt, the Cherethites and Pelethites, and the daughters of Zelophehad—all subjects for which I had not a minute to spare. During one of my triennial attacks of influenza, my second mistress brought a message from my deputy asking for enlightenment as to my views on the Hittites. I was ill to the verge of profanity and, turning my face to the wall literally—it was there already figuratively speaking—I replied, " Hang the Hittites." The return message was, " Nothing would give me greater pleasure." The duty of careful elimination presses on those who have to draw up syllabuses for one-period-a-week courses, and much depends on the judgment of the teacher. I am keen on the literary quality of

Holy Scripture, and I frequently pointed out the beauty of psalm or story, because I wanted the Bible to appear attractive. In order to make the stories seem more real I used to read over occasionally such chapters as that which tells of the bargaining for the Cave of Machpelah, or the Rebekah at the well episode, which portray scenes characteristic of Oriental life. Nevertheless I held firmly to the ideal of orderly knowledge of the main narrative— as a preparation for further study of the Bible.

In class, we—the class as a whole and myself—read alternative verses. This is a much quicker way of getting over the ground than by individual reading. Also, I was able to set the pace in emphasis and expression: the children imitated me, the result being a dramatic rendering where possible, and a suggestion of reverence by lowered tones, &c. It played a part in improving the children's reading. At times it was reverently funny. I remember the *whimper* in which Elijah was made to reply to the still, small voice. They were reading intensely and evidently thought the heroic prophet was unduly sorry for himself— a state of mind which they were taught to regard as below par. As they did no home work in Scripture and only very occasional home reading, I relied on this method to stimulate interest and memory. For home reading I gave only whole chapters or series of chapters. When the course required the selection and reading of only parts of chapters, we read them in class as described. For example, they read at home the series of chapters which describe the career of Joseph after his imprisonment, and I questioned them on the subject-matter. I always allowed open Bibles in question time—indeed, our Bibles were always open. To know how to search the Scriptures literally is almost as good as to know the text— you can always turn to what you want. Jacob's career we picked out in class and read alternately, also David's. Saul's lent itself easily to our system of home reading followed by questioning.

The girls came into the main school at the age of eleven. In the first year and form, they took a course of simple lessons on the Life of Our Lord, beginning at Bethlehem but following the lines of St. Mark's Gospel, with additions from the others as time permitted. Usually they were able to take all the incidents and parables. This course was needed to assure some orderly teaching of the most important part of the Bible to every child who came into the main school, even to those who left after only one year. In the second year I began the Old Testament. In Genesis, I gave as home reading the first two chapters and picked out and read in class the stories of the Babel and the Deluge, &c. After the twelfth chapter, we threaded our way through the history of the Jews. We had them settled in Canaan by the end of the first year, and in exile in Babylon by the end of the third. The fourth began with lessons on the life in Babylon, on Ezra and Nehemiah, with references to some of the prophecies. I gave three lectures on the period between the testaments and spent the last term of that year on a general survey of the Gospels, their characteristics and variation in content. The fifths read the Gospel of St. Luke and the Acts of the Apostles (when we could manage to get it in), and the sixth made good the deficiencies in the fifths and did a little work in the parts of the Scripture canon not taken elsewhere. I made what is best described as a series of elaborate allusions, accompanied by illustrative readings, to such books as the Psalms, the Wisdom books, the Epistles, the Apocalypse, &c., and, sometimes with the second year Sixth, I managed to read parts of *A Short History of Our Religion* (Somervell), which carries on the narrative to our own day. (I don't remember ever getting past the Reformation, but I hope the girls did so.) Indeed, as I enumerate all this, I am conscious that it will appear that I accomplished more than I did, but this book is a record of ideals striven for rather than of ideals attained. There was always much skimming and scrapping at the ends of the sessions. The girls left school with deep respect for the Bible and with some knowledge of its contents—that is all I am sure of.

I have said that the omissions necessary to such a course are important and need the exercise of judgment. Much of the books we ' studied ' were not even read. In Abraham's life, I took only his call, dealings with Lot, intercessory prayer for Sodom, the ' sacrifice ' of Isaac and, sometimes, the bargaining scene with Ephron the Hittite. Of the life of Jacob, only the birthright scene, his deception of his father, the visions, after which he was merged in the Joseph story. In Exodus, I read the first twelve chapters—with a flying leap over the period of the plagues—most of the wilderness incidents, the decalogue, and some few of the general domestic laws of the Mosaic code, and the description of the tabernacle with a design thereof. The contents of Leviticus I dismissed after explaining its name. I think I gave three lessons on parts of Numbers, deferring Deuteronomy—except the last chapter—to the later period to which it belongs. Judges I accepted where it stands, and read only the Deborah, Gideon, Jephthah, and Samson stories. As long as it did not interfere with the course, I left the order of books as it stands, Deuteronomy being excepted because of its prominence in the Life of Our Lord.

Deborah's song is convenient for the teaching of the characteristics of Jewish poetry: it is easily analysed and the parallelism is plain. I also used some of the variations in its text to explain the methods of compilers and translators, and it is an excellent starting-point for the introduction of the idea of progressive morality. Anthropomorphism I grappled with from the beginning and especially in Abraham's intercessory prayer. The Fosdick idea I developed in such stories as Jacob's visions, Elijah's strange experiences, &c. But the most important of all, the tracing of the progress in the knowledge of God, which underlies the entire teaching of the Old Testament, I kept in sight throughout, beginning with *Jehovah of Hosts*, passing through *Elohim* to the merciful and only God of Amos and right on through the Psalms to the " *Our Father* " of the Lord's Prayer. I quoted and misquoted what was originally a line from Dr. Fosdick's book until it assumed a rhythmical form:

> Did ever dubious morning twilight
> End in a more glorious noon?

My hope that these key thoughts would find a place in the memories of my pupils was based on this constant repetition. I was anxious to forestall the most ignorant of the criticism they were bound to encounter. I once heard a girl say that she thought my favourite Scripture characters were Amos, Balaam, and Jonah, and I know why she had received that impression—Amos, because of his advanced idea of God, and the other two because they are the *pièce de résistance* of the scoffer. The latter stories I classed together as alike in type and emphasis, and they illustrate many of the key ideas I was so anxious should penetrate.

I remember how hot with nervousness I was when, many years ago, I first used the word *legend* in connexion with the Old Testament stories. I gained courage to do so after reading a speech made, I think, by Dr. Armitage Robinson to the girls of the North London Collegiate school, a printed copy of which the late headmistress sent to me. Some young eyes opened wide when I first alluded to the similarity between the legends in Genesis and those of other ancient literatures. I held on for dear life to the Arthurian legends as adapted by Tennyson to express ideals of life: the parallel seems to me a close one between such work and that of the early compilers of the Bible stories. Nothing happened: I was too well known as a Bible-lover. Nevertheless, I was always on guard. I had not only to accustom the girls to modern ideas on the subject but also to give them facility in expression of the same—a reason for changed interpretations. Had I not recognized that a gradual modernization of Scripture teaching was not only necessary but overdue, I should have let well alone. To my own mind the wrappings of truth matter little and I believe that, to the waiting soul, truth is self-revealing in mysterious ways. There is no serious reason why a pious soul should not do what thousands have done, wrest spiritual consolation from a piece of political advice such as, " In quietness and in confidence shall be your strength ". I believe in the divine use of everyday incidents and commonplace utterances to convey His messages to listening souls, feeling sure that he that hath ears, hears. But the unintelligent way of regarding, say, Abraham as a saintly character instead of a pagan living up to his light and groping after truth, is in a different category, as is the old-fashioned way of reading meanings into irrelevant detail, as did the village preacher in Browning's *Christmas Eve*. Intelligent youth will not accept such misrepresentation.

But all this comes easily when one has once accepted as fact that a story may be imaginary in objective details and true in something deeper. It is all part of the apprehension of the spiritual in life. The lines:

> To me the meanest flower that blows can give
> Thoughts that do often lie too deep for tears

find an echo in the minds of many, but seem moonshine to the man described as follows:

> A primrose by the river's brim
> A yellow primrose was to him
> And it was nothing more.

The realization of the importance of the subjective and spiritual marks a distinct stage in the progress of soul-growing. The Bible is almost unintelligible to those who thus fail to find its hidden meaning.

Much later an incident occurred locally which is worth recording. The Students' Christian Union sent a band of university students to Snellham, and the distinguished professor who accompanied them preached in one of the chapels. In the course of the service, he addressed the children as follows: " I am going to tell you a true story which I know to be true because I made it up myself." He then related a charming and original story about an enchanted garden. I hastened to add this incident to my defensive armoury. Many of the girls had heard the address, and a better example of the embodying of truth in fiction could not have been devised. It remained for me to explain the mixture of truth and fiction in the Bible on the same lines.

It was with sincere regret that I felt obliged to explain to the Sixths that the so-called prophecies were not prophetic in the usual meaning of the term but merely topical. Much reverent sentiment has gathered round such poignantly beautiful words as, " He is despised and rejected of men, a man of sorrows and acquainted with grief ". I was quick to express the opinion that it is not only permissible but natural to adapt such beautiful poetic descriptions to Christ, Himself the Fairest among ten thousand, and that, in so doing, we are following the example of Mary of Bethany—bringing the distilled sweetness of human effort to lay at His feet. The date of the Psalms was another delicate matter. It had been so delightful to picture, say, the young poet-shepherd-king thinking out the twenty-third psalm while tending his flock. A counterbalance to such loss was provided by the interest gained in realizing how far advanced in the knowledge of God were the pious Jews in the centuries immediately before Christ, and we were able to make some simple but useful comparisons between the Greek seekers after God and their Jewish contemporaries.

I always began my lessons on the St. Luke Gospel by reference to the first two verses of the Epistle to the Hebrews, which bring out clearly the connexion between the revelation by the prophets and the supreme revelation of the Word made flesh. It is a thrilling experience to teach the life of Christ to eager and intelligent girls. The charm of the Gospels is unique. There is a holy stillness, a beautiful simplicity about the Gospel story. Everything in the narrative seems to reflect this charm: the home at Nazareth; the sermons on the hillside and by the lapping waters of the lake; the twilight healing of the sick and sad, when one forgets the crowd in contemplation of the quiet Figure of the Healer; the simple trust and quick obedience of " Follow Me. And he arose and followed Him "; the Bethany friendship and home life and perfume of spikenard very costly; the last supper and the precious intimate teaching that followed it; the dawn of the first Easter Day; even the " cloud that received Him out of their sight ". The restraint of the narrative, the directness of the Beatitudes and of those miniature masterpieces, the parables—all add to this

effect.   The very place names are musical: Galilee,
Nazareth, Bethany, Jerusalem, even Calvary, are full of
poetic suggestion.   In my own way, I profit from association with what is lovely.   I can well believe I benefited from these lessons as much as my pupils.   At one
time the exigencies of the timetable caused me to have
three lessons on the life of Christ on one day, and on my
way home, I used to feel that Snellham and Galilee were
not so far apart as I often felt them to be.

On the point of requiring children to learn passages
of the Bible by heart I did not come to any very definite
conclusion.   I shrank from hearing such passages as the
Beatitudes gabbled over by the children, and felt it to be
all-important that what is true and beautiful should not
be associated in any way with what is compulsory.   The
ideal is to induce children to learn voluntarily, and with a
little adroitness and much care in the hearing of the task,
I believe it might be managed.   I had one experience
which I should like to record, as showing how sensitive
to rhythm and expression even little children may be.
I had been telling the top form in the Preparatory—age
about ten—the story of the Jewish exile and how much
the exiles missed their beautiful temple.   I then recited
to them the psalm beginning: " By the rivers of Babylon,
there we sat down, yea we wept when we remembered
Sion ".   More to please myself—the incident took place
after the publication of a lecture by " Q " on the literary
beauty of the Bible in which he selected this passage for
special mention—than with any expectation of interesting
the class, I threw myself into the psalm, and as I was

saying the words " How can we sing the Lord's song in a
strange land?" I heard a little sigh. Glancing down immediately in front of me, I saw a little girl shake her head
sadly as though she was agreeing that it was *quite* out of
the question to sing under such circumstances. Four or
five years later, I was busy teaching the Fourth form
about the Exile and recommended them to read Psalm 137.
One of the class rose and offered to recite it, saying
she had learnt it after ' you recited it to us in the
Prep '. It was the child who had sighed and shaken
her head. Children vary immensely in sensitiveness to
beauty.

I found it advisable to supplement the ideas my girls
had formed about Christ from pictures and early lessons.
The idea of the ' gentle Jesus ' which is so effective in
winning the love of children for the ' Friend of little
children ' was one-sided, and I knew that the Snellham
ideal of character included strength as well as gentleness,
and that my girls would look for ideals of leadership,
force, courage. The average girl who plays games well
and learns to take knocks with the same fortitude as her
brothers, will be impressed when she realizes that Christ
spoke with authority, that He reversed current moral
values, upbraided the hypocrisy of His day, outwitted
those who tried to entangle Him in His talk, and set
His face steadfastly to go to Jerusalem. The willingness
to be a sport and not to play for safety were all part of
their everyday ideals, and they were impatient of what
they inelegantly termed ' sloppiness '.   Christianity
ought to attract youth, for Christ was a young man when

He went to His Cross; His religion calls to a life of adventure and achievement: there is nothing of slippered ease, of namby-pambyism, of elderly caution, about the Quest of the Holy Grail and the romantic following up to the Heights, and the hour is truly ' regal ' when the young Christian first mounts on guard. Oriental life is so much more deliberate than ours that I was always on my guard against leaving an impression of *elderliness*.

When I was teaching the Gospels I was anxious to present a lovable Christ to the girls. I avoided talking much about personal religion but threw my whole soul into the attempt to make them see that the religion of Christ is a winsome thing and that the Christian ideal is heavens above all others. Occasionally a girl would follow me into my room and ask questions arising out of the lessons—usually about prayer or faith. These questions I answered fully, for I do not believe in an inarticulate religion. I appreciate that there is an inarticulate morality which concerns itself with ' doing the decent thing and saying nothing about it '—admirable though possibly not stormproof—but I am unable to conceive of a Christ-lover who can keep quiet and refrain from speaking and acting on behalf of His kingdom.

School prayers form a practical part of religious in-struction and are a fine disciplinary influence. Some years ago, with many other headmistresses, I attended morning prayers at one of the most famous Public Schools for girls. The ceremonial—for so I must call it—pleased me. I admired the beautiful chapel, the rows of fine, well-groomed girls, the headmistress picturesque in gown and hood, her dignified conduct of the service, the organ music, singing and intoning, and joined happily in the service. Afterwards some of those with me commented on the aspect of the girls, which, they said, indicated a decorous boredom. Perhaps it is possible to oversublimate in the manner of services for the adolescent, and that we err in this direction by taking it for granted that what we enjoy ourselves is what they enjoy, or should enjoy. Environment plays a great part in creating what is usually called a devotional feeling, but is there not a risk lest, when familiarity has done its fatal work, that feeling may cease? Perhaps the safer way is to trust to other agencies than sense impressions, and that a simple lifting up of the heart to the Lord is the ideal worship. But how to ensure that our girls do so worship at the morning assembly?

I came to the conclusion that it is best that girls should take a very active share in the school forms of worship or inevitably it will seem to belong to the hierarchy and they will lose interest in it. On no account should anything occur, either during the service or in preparation for it, which conveys the impression that it is a kind of meaningless function or a school show. With something approaching horror, I have come across people who think it right to correct faults in the singing or reading at prayers. Whether the correction takes place before, during, or after the prayers it is bound to divert the attention from the true aim of worship, the ' practice of the Presence of God '. Also, I came to see a similar risk in the presence of strangers on the platform unless they conducted the service or delivered a relevant address.

In accordance with my principle in school organization—to impose as little as possible, to guide rather than to dominate—I tried to give the girls a practical share in the arrangement and conduct of the service. The forms took it in turn to choose the hymn which was sung every morning of the five days of the week. This impressed the hymns on their minds: I used to notice that many of the first-formers who stood in the front used to sing by heart on Friday morning. I adopted a hymn book, published by Messrs. Harrap, which was written, possibly, for boys—a fact which made it the more interesting for my girls—and which gave at the end of each hymn a few details about the writer, including the school at which he was educated, the whole conveying an impression of school life which I valued highly. The book included not only Wesley and Watts at their best, but lyrics from Palgrave, Whittier, Clough, and other moderns. Each girl had a hymn book given to her on entering the school, her name being written in it by myself, and I was surprised at the affection with which the little shabby volumes came to be regarded. We read the Bible together—alternate verses—once a week. While they were turning over pages to find the passage, in a short sentence or two I tried to convey some idea of the context, and again, in identically the same words, when all was quiet and the reading about to begin. Chapters taken at random are hard to grasp, unless one knows one's Bible well. (I marvel at the stolidity of congregations listening to mumbled reading of what they would find it hard to understand if they themselves were reading the text.) I wanted my girls to see Christ as He moved along the road or taught on the hillside; to realize as we read the thirteenth chapter of first Epistle to the Corinthians, or from one of the Epistles to Timothy, that, here again, it was a teacher and pupils; that the God we were now seeking was the same that made David strong and Jeremiah's lonely life heroic. To make children think about what they are reading is the only way to secure reverence in school worship—a reverence that is worth the name. Occasionally in the same way I described the content of the hymn to be sung and found a quiet word on one or other of the petitions of the Lord's Prayer effective in preventing the thoughtless rattling through of a prayer so familiar. If I were beginning again, I should compose and use a simple *bidding* prayer, which would give the girls exactly the kind of share in the praying that I wished them to have. I do not believe in long, or in what are called literary prayers: they pass over the heads of young worshippers or divert attention to their style. Heartfelt prayers, I incline to think, are simple and to the point. The average duration of the time we devoted to morning worship was about twelve minutes, and I had to concentrate on the essentials of worship if this short time was to prove what old-fashioned theologians used to call a means of grace.

Teaching Scripture to children of preparatory age was quite a different matter and presented no serious problems. Our Preparatory was a late development and, although it entailed special responsibilities, in retrospect I see how whole-heartedly I enjoyed my intercourse with the little children. At first I was not a success with them, but later, so I am credibly informed, I became so popular that the children chortled with joy when I was sighted coming up the garden path of their annexe and, if volume of sound is any criterion, their welcoming ' Good morning ' was heartfelt. The change took place after I had been reading a book on child psychology, in which the writer stated that anyone who succeeded in smiling at a baby so effectively as to elicit an answering smile, was the means of releasing pent-up energy in the infant, and thus doing it a kindness. This commended itself to me as a cheap and easy way of benefiting the rising generation, and I can state truthfully that I have tried the effect of my smile on hundred of the babies who have come my way and evoked very many little three-cornered, toothless (or nearly so) smiles. When my efforts had the opposite effect as (alas!) sometimes happened, I fell back on the thought that ' it is not what man does but what man Would Do ', &c.

In describing my attempts at religious instruction in the Preparatory, I must explain that the lesson period began as a *lesson* but usually ended as a *symposium*. Free discussion was allowed, provided that only one person spoke at a time, and, in practice, I succeeded in reserving the right to intervene if this rule was not kept. The psychic atmosphere of the Prep. was favourable to oratory and I rose to the occasion, returning to the Big School, heckled, heated, and happy. Never, for instance, did I finish up the Goliath story—the most dramatic in my repertory—without what the newspapers call, tumultous applause; the children clapped and stamped wildly at the poetic justice (we did not call it by that name, but probably, ' the crowning joke ') of Goliath's head being cut off by Goliath's own sword. The boys, true to the young barbarian type, liked the fighting stories best; the girls, if given a choice, invariably preferred Moses because, as a scrap of a girl explained, ' he begins by being a baby '. It was, however, a little girl that made the most bloodthirsty remark I ever heard of during the course of a long life. The lesson was on the Mount Carmel, the Jehovah - versus - Baal story, when the priests of Baal are represented as building an altar and sacrificing a bullock on it. A little girl asked whether a bullock was the same as a bull, and received the reply that a bullock was ' a little bull '. When, at the end of the lesson, an attempt was made to justify the wholesale slaughter of the priests of Baal, by explaining that they had led the people into idolatry, the little girl who had asked about the bullock exclaimed triumphantly, " Serve them right for killing that dear little bull."

The symposium type of lesson leads to much self-revealing on the part of the pupil-participants, and I was not always able to account for eccentricities of utterance and behaviour. One boy, a wee Scot, used to refuse to look at me during the lesson and sat crumpled up, with bowed head and eyes glued to the table. When the lesson began he was in his normal position, but, in a minute or two, curled up and remained so until I was on the point of leaving. Any attempt to make him sit up seemed to lacerate his feelings so sorely that I desisted from the attempt and taught literally over his head. Whether this was due to personal dislike of me or my subject, or to that sensitiveness to whatever impinges on theology which is said to be characteristic of the Scotch mentality, I shall never know. The following incident may throw light on the problem. At the end of his second year (age eight plus), I was giving a lesson on the ten commandments and was toning down the Jewishness of the fourth in some such words as the following: " Of course it is not wrong to do necessary work on the sabbath, like nursing the sick and looking after the animals on a farm," when we were startled by a shout which would have made rafters ring, and which flung defiance at me in the words, " *And get the dinner yeddy (sic)* "—it was the little Scot sitting up rigidly and glaring at me. I believe he was blaming me for the decalogue and making a desperate effort to save his Sunday dinner from my iconoclastic activities. I reassured him and he curled up comfortably again. Another boy was curiously interested in roofs. I had noticed this peculiarity for some time and had made superfluous references to roofs to note the reaction. He was wildly excited when Rahab took the spies up to the roof, stood up at his desk and exclaimed that she was a sharp woman to think of covering them with flax stalks after she had made them lie down on the flat roof. When Achish, towards the end of David's outlawry, gave him the town of Ziklag to live in, Harry exclaimed, " At last the poor chap got a roof to cover his head," adding with a chuckle, " as many roofs as he liked." He made minute inquiries about the roofing of temple and tabernacle, and was contemptuous of the latter as not ' being much good ', and when we came to the story of the paralytic being let down through the roof, Harry marched out, walked across the room to the window from which the lofty Gothic building of the ' Big School ' was visible, and, without more ado, proceeded to deliver a very intelligent address—about a minute long—on roofs, gutters, slates, pipes and their uses. We listened quietly until he finished and resumed his seat with a sigh of happiness which, I believe, came from the depths of his being. I failed to discover any reason for this harmless preoccupation, his father being a professional man.

When the children felt it necessary to set me right on any subject on which they felt better informed than I was, they did so with the most perfect consideration for my feelings. I was once beginning the birthright story and had just described Esau as Jacob's elder brother when an insinuating little voice interrupted: " I think, Miss Cleeve, they were twins *to begin with*." The qualifying phrase, I feel sure, was used to spare my feelings which a direct contradiction might have wounded. For many years I had explained the meaning of a symbol by reference to the ring in marriage. I was caught out at last. " You see, children," I was saying, " a ring has no end and it means that the love of the bridegroom for the bride will have no end," when a gentle voice said, " *I'm not sure* that it hasn't—are you, Miss Cleeve?" It is rather difficult to find a good specimen of a symbol which all children would recognize. I believe I fell back on a handshake.

Boys are different from girls in their way of looking at things. They are more direct in their questions and think about the answers more carefully. A girl tends to accept what is said to her: boys weigh it up. The Snellham boys were always angry when a girl came one over them: I think they were not sure that they were not attending a school intended for girls and they were concerned, subconsciously, about their dignity. I remember one funny little burst of wrath on the part of a boy who was in his last preparatory stage and feeling superior in consequence. Apropos of Daniel, a girl asked me how many lions it took ' to make a den '. I answered about a dozen. The boy sitting near to me shook his head and said, " Oh no, Miss Cleeve, God couldn't shut the mouths of twelve lions at once." " Yes, He could," said the girl, " He can do everything, can't He, Miss Cleeve?" " Then why doesn't He shut their mouths before they open them?" flashed Harvey, crimson with wrath. I refrained from reply, and to change the subject asked how many of those present had seen a lion. This drew forth such a number of tall stories—for nothing inflames a child's imagination more than the idea of wild beasts—that I hurriedly applied the closure and the class ended on a less cheerful note than usual.

When they came to school these children were already little Christ-lovers: hymns about a tender Shepherd and pictures of a gentle Jesus had done their work. During my recital of His doings, they sided with Him volubly and

passionately. " It wasn't playing the game," exploded
one boy—the hero of my last story it was—with angry
tears in his eyes when I was describing the attempt to
entangle Him in talk by showing Him a coin and asking
an awkward question. So scornful were they of the disciples ' who all forsook Him and fled ' that I judged it
wise to counter their assurances that under no circumstances whatever would they have done the like, by reminding them that it was open to them to prove their
loyalty here and now. St. Peter they handled so roughly
that it bordered on irreverence, and I stressed the fact
that he ' went out and wept bitterly ', after which one of
them remarked judicially, " Well, that's *something*."   I
have told children the story of the trial before Pilate
scores of times, but never, so far as memory serves,
without having attention diverted to eager inquiries as
to what Pilate's wife had dreamt—they wanted more
details. The first time I was off my guard and absent-
mindedly on the point of answering, " She dreamt she
had spots of blood on her hand." On consideration, I
came to understand this unconscious twist of thought to
Lady Macbeth, for there are points of similarity between
the two episodes, although one is fact, the other the
highest fiction; one the prose of a miserably sordid scene,
the other the poetic revealing of a soul at war with itself.
In both we discern the throes of spiritual struggle; both
Procula and Lady Macbeth seek to influence their hus-
bands; in both cases, the crime-ridden conscience takes
refuge in a weak symbolism. Pilate washes his hands
literally in the Prætorium at Jerusalem; Lady Macbeth

in a troubled dream phantasy in the castle at Dunsinane.

The Bible stories undoubtedly charm the minds of children because they seem to be of real life. Most of my children liked ' true stories best '. I remember a boy who was making such slow progress in reading that I undertook to have him over daily to read to me. The first day he read from a volume of fairy tales and the reading was halting and unsatisfactory. Next day, he marched into my room, came close up to me and said in a coaxing tone, " Miss Cleeve, need I read out of that silly book again?" " What's wrong with the book?" I asked. He made a gesture indicative of nausea, and said, " I don't like fairies; there's *nothing to them*. Please let me read about something *sensible*—like caterpillars." I sent for a natural history primer and the course of John's reading ran smoothly ever after. I have my fears for John: he will achieve success in business, may even become the mayor of his native Snellham and be knighted for his services to his political party—the conservative. But he will always think that common sense rules the world—which it doesn't—and that business is business—which it isn't.

My work in teaching Scripture in Snellham was made much easier because the girls attended Sunday schools. Almost at the first lesson I was able to spot those who did not, and made a point of commending these schools, for which I came to have a great respect, and it was a satisfaction to me that the majority of my Sixth Form were Sunday school teachers before they ceased to be school-

girls. The knowledge these schools impart is necessarily
confused but makes a good foundation.   In Sunday
schools the atmosphere is the important thing, and for
tens of thousands of children they provide the only
opportunity for christian culture. I shall not be surprised
if, when the Master of our schools arranges His departments in order of achievement, Sunday schools come out
top, for that Master is the Christ who told us that ' it is
not the will of your Heavenly Father that one of these
little ones should perish '.   During the war I heard of a
naval chaplain who asked religious teachers of the young
to instruct them in some form of prayer: he had so often
been asked by sailors for a prayer to use in case they were
torpedoed. The godlessness and superstition of such a
request appalled me.   Sunday school scholars are accustomed to simple prayers, often extempore, and many of
their hymns are prayers.   No ex-Sunday school scholar
but would know how to find his way to the Eternal
Father strong to save. There is a real need for such
schools to supplement the services of the church, which
are often unintelligible to the indifferently educated, and
the much-discussed religious teaching which in many
schools is seriously handicapped. The christian church
depends on the Sunday school for much of the nurture
of young christians.   How is it that such work is hampered by the lack of well-qualified teachers? How comes
it that so many graduate and college-trained teachers fail
to bring their gifts into the treasury of the church and are
not to be found teaching in the Sunday school?   That
work has special attractions for the young and chivalrous

Christ-lover: it involves the sacrifice of a delicious bit of leisure; there is no kudos attached to it; it is a service of love for Love's sake, eagerly to be undertaken by those who ' seek no other guerdon

> Except to share the travail
> That makes Christ's kingdom come.'

CHAPTER VIII

The General Curriculum

There are many opinions as to the true function of a school and as to what constitutes real success in school-keeping. As to the first I was never in doubt as far as my own experience extends. A school is a place to which the young human animal is sent in order that he may receive a certain kind of training which is not to be had else-where. A child learns naturally and happily from his environment, but there are many aspects of life which do not reveal themselves to the mere observer and cannot be learnt by observation alone. Moreover, there are in him latent powers which the common experiences of life do not develop. The function of the school is to intro-duce the child to community life, to open the avenues of his mind to all sides of life, to train his mind to apprehend and reason—in a word to *think*—and his body to be a fit instrument for this developed personality to function through.

Everything in school life depends on this development of the power of thought and on the opening out of the great avenues of the mind. Home and its environment play a most important part in education which grows gradually less as the child takes his place in the life of the race. The business of a day school is not to reproduce home conditions but to supplement them. I have heard a school described as a place of leisure. I do not regard it so. Leisure is desirable and necessary, but school should be a place of work—happy, intelligent work. The normal, healthy child enjoys work, and is at his best when busily employed. A certain amount of freedom for those who are old enough to use it wisely may be desirable in some cases, but for leisure and rest the home is the place. I have also come across those who maintain that schools ought to provide amusement for the children. I agree with this view of a school's function, but should limit the so-called ‘ amusement ’ to what exercises the thinking faculty. The power to think conduces to happiness, even in small children. I made a point of observing children of kindergarten age when they were listening to the senior school recite, or seeing them act parts of the plays of Shakespeare. Those who watched and wondered were the happy ones of the audience: they were just beginning to think, and finding the process all engrossing. One result of our national bias to action rather than thought is that thinking is not regarded as pleasurable and the thoughtless child is looked upon as the normal one. I am not sure that this is so. In my opinion a school is not successful unless the young people it sends out into the world are capable of thinking things out and find the process of so doing enjoyable, and who are alive on all sides to what is worth thinking about. The world is so full of a number of things capable of making us happy as kings, and ability to appreciate them is the result of good training, whether received in or out of school.

I am sorry to say that my school failed in this respect. Our English education fails in much the same way. At school my girls were healthy and happy; they passed their examinations creditably, a fair proportion going on to various universities. Their games record was creditable and, as a whole, they were of the kind described as *capable*. Nevertheless, I now see that their education had failed in one most important respect: it had not gone far enough. When education has gone far enough those who have drunk of its refreshing waters are still athirst. My girls were sorry to leave school, but many of them threw down their books with a sigh of relief—as tools for which they had no further use.

When I expressed these opinions to a fellow head-mistress she replied that we must reconcile ourselves to this partial failure because the English are doers rather than thinkers. That is true. Is it always to be so? Are thinking and doing as incompatible as we believe? In extreme cases I grant that they may be, but I feel sorry that our education does not produce the ideal combination—the practical man who is also a thinker. My patriotism will not allow me to make comparisons, but I believe that the two are to be found in combination, and that ultimately the real power—I do not mean sovereignty—will rest with the nation which can both think and do. Our education fails somewhere.

I once set out to climb a mountain. Nature, I must

explain, intended me to amble along the level, she having denied me an effective physical apparatus for climbing. But sojourning among climbers and listening to their talk was so furiously tantalizing that, one morning, I set off to climb one of the easiest of the Cumbrian Fells. As I had been warned, I found the beginning of the ascent rugged and stony. After a bit of hard going, things became easier and hopes were high. I sat down to rest and refresh myself for the final struggle when—a mist came down and forced me to give up the attempt. I came down without having seen the extensive view which was my objective.

Something analogous to this takes place in school education. The going is hard at first. Our unphonetic spelling and lack of a decimal system make preparatory work heavy. Then the beginnings and outline work in the various subjects, even when taught by modern and attractive methods, kindle only a childish enthusiasm. When preliminaries are over and a good foundation laid— when we have reached the stage when intelligent appreciation is possible—then examination pressure begins, and ends, only too often, when the pupil closes the school door behind him for the last time. Our boys and girls never get close enough to knowledge to feel its attractiveness. As well expect a man to fall in love with a woman in whom he sees no charm as expect our youth to delight in the kind of knowledge acquired during examination preparation.

" Studies," says Lord Bacon, speaking of what we call book-learning, " serve for delight, for ornament, and for ability." He put ' delight ' first, and the chief problem of education within the school building is to see that this order is kept. Dull teaching is not the only cause of listless learning. Some subjects such as natural science interest the normal child from the first; others, given time and a free hand, become increasingly delightful. Latin is not among these as far as the ordinary pupil of an ordinary school is affected. I incline to believe that the point of *delight* is rarely reached in the study of Latin in municipal schools, and that gerund-grinding is partly responsible for the general failure of our education to ' serve for delight '. I find it hard to believe in the intellectual honesty of those who maintain that the study of the classics in the average municipal school, with the usual crowded curriculum, leads to a realization of the glory of Greece and the grandeur of Rome. My opinion is that it creates a prejudice against not only itself, but also all ' studies ', leading therefore to neither glory nor grandeur but direct to mediocrity. Intelligent boys and girls will never enjoy unintelligent grind, and, however we may sugar the pill by direct or indirect methods, the learning of grammar is a dusty business to be carried on only for the sake of future pleasure or profit. When the profit is small compared with the expenditure of effort and time (five periods out of thirty-five it was with us) and the pleasure is never realized, it becomes dangerous to force such blind-alley studies upon our children. It would be interesting to know how many of our pupils are really compensated in after life for their long efforts to learn Latin. I once heard what I consider the most ingenuous—

not to say *ingenious*—argument in favour of compulsory Latin in schools. It was adduced by a learned professor of Latin in the Arts Theatre of the university in which he lectured. He said it was good for people to study something which brought them nothing in return. Nothing for something is a fine ideal—for those who can afford it.

I have before me an essay on a subject akin to this which speaks of the " picked *thousand* of English men and women, who, year by year, base their culture on Hellenic inspiration ". Is a knowledge of the Greek language necessary for that inspiration? If I thought so, I should hesitate to express these opinions lest I should be advocating the closing of an avenue to what is pre-eminently desirable. I am not of that opinion. Great as is the world's indebtedness to Greece and Rome, in another direction Hebrew thought has had a still wider influence. We do not insist on the study of Hebrew in order that our pupils may benefit from Hebraic inspiration, nor does anyone doubt the adequacy of our translations from the Hebrew scriptures. I see no reason why Hellenic inspiration should not be conveyed in the same way, and for that reason should be glad if the time and effort now expended on grammatical grind were devoted to the reading of translations and the study of classical history.

I regret that I made no effort to arrange for this in my school. I have before me a little book which would have served them well as the accompaniment to a study of classical history. It contains some two hundred pages of extracts from twenty-four classical authors, trans-

lated into excellent English by a number of translators.
The extracts are well chosen. The first is the oath which
Greek youth took when they were registered as citizens—
Ephebi: " I will leave my country not less but greater
and more powerful than when she is committed to me."
I should have liked my girls to have at hand the story of
the parting of Hector and Andromache as translated by
Lang, Leaf, and Myers, and to know about the gracious
white-armed Nausicaa's hospitality to Odysseus, and how
she said:

> Far off we dwell
> Loved by the gods and zoned by the deep sea.
> Now comes this wanderer—let us treat him well;
> All strangers and all poor by Zeus are sent
> And love can make a little gift excel;

and how Socrates died after praying that he might be
made " beautiful in soul ". I feel sure that they would
have rejoiced over Cory's exquisite translation of Calli-
machus's lament over the death of his poet friend:

> I wept as I remembered how often you and I
> Had tired the sun with talking, and sent him down the sky.
> . . . .
> Still are thy pleasant voices, thy nightingales, awake,
> For Death he taketh all away but them he cannot take;

and over Byron's translation of Catullus's ode over Les-
bia's dead bird. The girl guides would have been interested in Calverley's translation of the description of the
camp fires before Troy:

As in the heights of heaven the moon shines clear and around
   her
Shine in their beauty the stars, nor is one cloud moving in
   ether;
Shines forth every cliff, and the jutting peaks and the head-
   lands,
Forest and glen; then—as opens the rifting firmament heaven-
   wards
Star is revealed upon stars; and gay is the heart of the herds-
   man.
Not less in number than they, from Xanthus' stream to the
   sea sands,
Glimmered the red watchfires that compassed Ilion alway,
Glimmered amid Troy's host as a thousand stars; and at each
   one,
There sat threescore and ten, their faces lit up by the fire.

The history mistresses would have been glad of the extracts from Cæsar, Tacitus, Pliny, Livy, Sallust, and the
English mistresses' task of explaining classical allusions
in poem, play, and essay made easier. I am conscious
that I am dogmatizing from a limited experience, but,
in my own mind, am convinced that by the reading of
even such snippets—to say nothing of the more con-
tinuous reading which might follow—a deeper appreciation of the great debt that civilization owes to Greece
and Rome would result.

Two reasons are adduced by those who, while admitting
that much of the compulsory study of Latin is barren of
result, are yet unwilling to cut it out. They say that even
a slight familiarity with Latin and a little practice in con-
struing, leads to greater precision in the use of the mother

tongue. This is undoubtedly the case. Against the loss in this direction, must be set the gain in time for other literary studies and the lessened strain on the curriculum. The question must be answered according to circumstances, and no one having felt the value of a classical training will decide against it without much heart-searching.

The second reason given by those who agree with me that compulsory Latin often leads nowhere is that grind strengthens growing minds. It may well be so. We should all have tauter muscles if we took to practising Sandow's exercises whenever we had a minute to spare— but how dull! How we should come to detest such exercises! and possibly physical drill of all kinds. When staying at a pension in Normandy in my (very) salad days, I was confronted at déjeuner with a dish which I did not recognize, but later found to be a globe artichoke. Unsuspectingly I helped myself to some of the inedible, fluffy centre, filling my mouth with something too dry to be swallowed or even salivated. The sequel was humiliating. Transferred to mental processes, this is what happens when children in municipal schools are made to study Latin: they find it too dry to swallow.

I shrank from taking steps to abolish Latin from the main curriculum in my school and held on to it as long as I dared. The post-war extension of the free place system caused a rush of clever but, in spite of an abundance of the three R's, quite uneducated children into the school. The teaching of a second foreign language was soon seen to be impracticable, even absurd. Taking my courage in both hands, I cut Latin out, retaining it only in the Sixth Literary, where it was studied for two or three years in preparation for the universities. When I reported my action to the governors and overheard one say to another, " Latin never did anybody any good," I suffered a violent revulsion of feeling: truly I had allied myself with the hateful Philistine. My action was approved, the only dissentient following me out of the room to suggest that the absence of Latin from a school education might be a social hindrance to Snellham girls already handicapped in that way by living in an industrial town. That feeling remains a factor in the situation: convention is a powerful force in middle-aged minds. Perhaps the rising generation when their day of power comes will refuse to be bound by such shackles. Meanwhile we may reflect that Shakespeare had little Latin and less Greek and made excellent use of translations.

In the early days of my headship, when the school was small and too poor to pay for advanced work, I used to teach the few girls who were aiming at a university career both Greek and Latin after school hours on what was virtually an intensive system, as we managed to secure successes in the London Intermediate Arts examination after two years' work in both languages. When I introduced the system at Snellham I had no doubt about its practicability. My plan of action was as follows: for the first month of the school session, the matriculants in the last school examination spent more than half their time on Latin grammar, other subjects being held up partially to allow of this. In the first two or three lessons I explained the formation and function of the Latin cases, after which the girls worked through an exhaustive set of exercises specially arranged for the purpose, answers being entered alongside the questions. I started them off on these tests but, as soon as I felt only practice was needed, I left them to check one another. Mutual help and sociability were great factors in the success of the method. By the end of the first week the declensions were above suspicion; in another fortnight a test paper was worked on adjectives and pronouns. Verbs were tackled in the same way. By the half-term they had a working knowledge of Latin accidence and were soon reading ' set books ' as easily as though they had learned Latin in the main school. They passed the supplementary School Certificate in that subject the following July, and took it to the subsidiary stage in the Higher Certificate a year later. We worked on these lines several years without any examination failures.

I have taught Latin more often on the usual than on the intensive system. The two methods are entirely dissimilar and the latter needs safeguarding in several ways or disaster will follow. The girls must be keen and clever —one slow-witted girl spoils the class. They must understand what is happening and join in wholeheartedly. When I introduced the system, it was quite usual for undergraduates at colleges to take up a new subject in the intermediate year and pass an examination in it at the end of session. When I explained to the girls that I was treating them as undergraduates, they were gratified and a sporting element was introduced which roused interest in the cramming and turned gerund-grinding into a game. At the first sign of muddle-headedness, the teacher must call a halt. It is *absolutely essential* to make sure of every step of the advance: the system fails and fails badly if this is not done. Most of the girls I taught seemed to enjoy this intellectual steeplechase. I should not advise the method in case of girls or teachers who are not inclined to take risks and make sprints. Also there must be perfect co-operation between teacher and taught, and mistresses of the old type may find it too revolutionary to attempt. As I have said, my first staff were successful, everything going according to schedule. Later there were difficulties, either because the girls were not all keen-witted or the mistress too slow and prolix— unable to understand that there is a time for everything, even for cramming.

Our compensation for the loss of Latin was great, although not exactly what I should have liked it to be. The amount of home work necessary was excessive, and I felt it right to use the periods formerly assigned to Latin in allowing time for ' home work ' in school. I distributed the five periods so that it was possible for a periodical exercise in every subject to be worked under the supervision of the specialist at school, the only exception being the English essays in forms five and four. These exercises, which were collected and corrected by the supervising mistress, came to be an excellent test of the girls' progress. There were other advantages: the staff knew what amount of written work had to be corrected— so much and no more. This was a safeguard against

much ineffective correcting in the case of over-con-
scientious mistresses and a check on the negligence of
others. Henceforth, the only home work (properly so
called) allowed was twenty minutes' preparation for each
subject in the next day's timetable. When I had made
this rule, I had to leave the observance of it to the girls
and their parents. I was aware that the girls did not
always limit themselves to the allowance, but felt sure
that, in general, my wishes would be honoured and for-
bore to inquire lest untruth should result. I came to the
conclusion that, as long as circumstances alter cases,
control of home work in day schools is impossible to
maintain.

Language work was not a strong feature in my school,
but, for a short time and under a very clever mistress,
French once became a most popular subject. The human
instrument is important in the teaching of living language, and there is much individuality about French—
the *Frenchiness* of a teacher making a great impression in
favour of the language. A dull teacher of phonetics is
a calamity in a school: a prejudice against the subject is
created. Teachers of phonetics need to prepare their
lessons very carefully. Indeed, I came to realize that a
teacher's preparation of the method of handling her
lesson is often more important than her preparation of
the matter.

My first French specialist stayed with us into the teens
of years and was then absorbed by the war-time need for
French-speaking Englishwomen. She was vigorous and
alive to her finger tips and this quality was reflected in her

teaching. We did no very advanced work, but the girls enjoyed their lessons, passed their examinations without worrying about them, and in time came to lose that peculiar shyness which—*then* more than *now*—afflicts the Britisher who is trying to speak a foreign language in his own country. She cajoled girls into talking French whenever opportunity offered, and I was delighted to hear it on staircase and in corridor, as well as in class room. They played games and acted in French, made little speeches without nervousness, and listened intelligently to French lectures which I was able to provide for them every now and again. An inspector complained whimsically that he could not induce the girls of a certain form to answer him in English, and certainly there was great determination not to be beaten in the struggle to make themselves intelligible. This mistress's methods were her own. When the direct method was being discussed, she refused to adopt it—much to my dismay, as I was, like most inexperienced headmistresses, anxious to be up-to-date. I believe she was too direct for the direct method: she knew how to get what she wanted and was afraid of beating the air. When the Full Inspection came along, as a sop to Cerberus she gave some lessons in the direct method and was criticized to me as being slavishly addicted to it, for by that time it was generally recognized as needing dilution and much supplementing. The craze for it certainly went too far, but the net effect was good: French teaching in this country has never been so stolidly English as it was before the direct method became the vogue. Educational progress is made in that ebb and flow fashion. A new method is started and talked about until the reform, like a great tidal wave, threatens to overwhelm existing conditions and all but the steadiest are affected. Then the tide turns, and, by and by, only a rich alluvial deposit remains. I remember the anti-examination craze when I believed the educational millenium was at hand. The wave receded, leaving, as its deposit, a reorganized system of Secondary School examinations. Thus will it be with the Montessori and Dalton methods: they may not be generally adopted, but how rich their deposit in child study and freedom! One practical disadvantage of these reactions is that amateur educationists become aware of the wave only after the ebb has begun and the ' talking ' has to begin all over again. Schoolmasters and mistresses are given to discussion, and some seem to think that the main thing is to ' get a move on ' anyhow and in any direction. Meanwhile the human child varies little. The English schoolboy in this twentieth century is probably much the same as the urchin that plagued old Orbilius, his predecessors and successors throughout the centuries, and educational method changes slowly because its human material remains practically unchanged.

I have always resented the cramping influence on teaching which examination preparation exerts and, when the anti-examination wave was at its height, should have abolished examinations in my school, had it not been that my colleague, the headmaster of the Snellham Municipal Boys' School, declined to do so, and we usually acted together in matters of that kind. I lived to be thankful for a check which kept me from serious blundering. The plight of those schools which had reorganized their curricula without having regard to examination requirements was serious when the Board made them compulsory. I learnt discretion from that headmaster, although our educational outlook differed in every direction. He kept the even tenor of his way unmoved by movements, reforms, inspectorial reports, and what not, demolishing them all, in conversation with me, by the use of the word *bunkum*—which came to be my private name for him. Dr. Johnson is credited with saying that nobody can teach anybody anything. In practice my colleague agreed with him, for his method of 'teaching' consisted in *making boys learn*. With considerable freedom in the manner of the *making*, all teaching amounts to that in the end. I notice that Snellham 'old boys', many of whom passed brilliantly through their university courses and now occupy important positions, rise up and call their headmaster blessed for *making them learn*, and am confirmed in my belief that the wisest school discipline is concerned with preventing children from wasting their time and committing follies during the irresponsible years.

My second French specialist was a contrast to her predecessor. Herself a perfect blend of French and English nationalities, she taught *charmingly*—Snellham girls were sensitive to charm—as well as powerfully. I have elsewhere described her skilful management of classes. Under her, the advanced work prospered. For the only time in my experience the most advanced girls in the

Literary Sixth translated into French with some regard for the *style* of the French they wrote. After she left, the standard rarely rose above the requirements of the Higher Certificate examination.

The study of modern languages would be made easier and more attractive if an international arrangement for the interchange of intending teachers could be made— an extension of the Board's present system of *assistantes* in schools. To have only English people teaching foreign languages is a waste of time and effort. One young foreigner per hundred pupils would be needed to make the arrangement effective. I can picture to myself groups of girls enjoying informal talks with such novel companions, going for walks with them, acting little French plays under their guidance, and learning to speak French naturally and pleasantly as they did all this. It would then be easy to form French ' circles ' and a French atmosphere would be created. My ideal arrangement would be an English teacher for grammatical work and translation into English, a foreigner for conversational and recreative work, and a division between the two for composition in the foreign language, each senior form writing ' compositions ' for both. The study of foreign languages would then, I feel sure, ' serve for delight '. My girls enjoyed intercourse with their *correspondantes* and reading French magazines, but French always remained a very foreign language.

When I began my work in Snellham, the small staff were all of the form mistress type, and specialists were engaged, one by one, as numbers increased. I believe in the specialist system: it enables the Head to assign responsibility more definitely, and responsibility ministers to happiness by satisfying the will to power. But before it was adopted, it fell to me to eke out the various subjects at need. I found this Jack-of-all-trades kind of life very trying and owe a debt of gratitude to the man (I feel sure it was a *man*) who first invented keys —especially mathematical ones. There, however, one advantage—I gained experience in the teaching of many subjects and, in education, any experience is better than none. I formed the opinion that history is the easiest subject to teach badly and the hardest to teach well. History teachers have not only to make dry bones live, but to reconstruct the skeleton and endow it with personality. The three essentials for the successful teaching of history are a power of discrimination of essentials, a feeling for the picturesque, and dramatic power. Our syllabus was the usual one. In the first year, we read Miss Synge's *Story of the World*, which came in usefully in Scripture—I was always so relieved not to have to fumble with atlases when Abraham had to be brought from Mesopotamia to Canaan and then sent down to Egypt—and in English Literature. Then began a two-year study of the outlines of our own island story. I insisted on orderly knowledge, and in the fourth form we began the examination period—the latest period allowed by the regulations along with contemporary European history (when additions to the options made the combination possible). The besetting sin of the history mistress is the dictation of notes, which I consider permissible only to relieve external examination pressure.

History is one of the two most cultural subjects in the Secondary School curriculum and, if properly taught, should have a practical influence on adult thought, one indication of which would be that clap-trap would be recognized for what it is. Some knowledge of the experiments, achievements and blunders of our forefathers is essential for balanced judgment in national affairs. It is of national importance that history should be well taught, not to the few but to all. It is the outline work that stands in the way of a really interesting intensive study. We have been a nation a very long time from the history teacher's point of view: there is so much to teach and not much time to give. It will be a great day when the cinema for educational purposes assumes its rightful place. Then will the process and pageantry of our great story be placed before our children, and well-annotated and well-chosen films discover the doings of the past for the sake of the present generation. The ground will then be cleared for detailed study of great movements and developments which have special interest for the present. I can picture the enthusiasm of intelligent youth when reading the work of specialists in certain periods of history—the rise of representative government and life story of the mother of parliaments; the coming of the Friars; the Reformation and history of Puritanism; the Renaissance and so forth. Luxury reading—Chesterton's *St. Francis*, Drinkwater's plays, Shaw's *St. Joan*, &c.— will be possible. I have noticed a tendency for history examination papers to require answers which are virtually short essays. I hope the time will come when history examination papers will consist wholly of a wide choice of essays on such subjects as I have alluded to. There is a thrill in history, and our pupils if rightly taught will respond enthusiastically.

Geography I always regard as the handmaid of history, and here again will the educational film shorten the learning of outlines and introduce a living interest. The importance of this subject grows in proportion to the extension of facilities for transit and as internationalism develops. Future generations will be cosmopolitan.

Natural science ought to ' serve for delight ' from the very first lesson, for scientific knowledge satisfies that natural curiosity which is sometimes classed as a primary instinct. If science does not interest, the fault lies in the teaching. Our children do not concern themselves about the Norman Conquest or yearn to have the ablative explained to them, but they do want to know how the wireless works and why some things float in the bath water and others don't. I have lived without the interest of science, and realize what an important avenue of the mind is opened by such scientific training as we now provide in a liberal education. I recognize good science teaching when I see it. In our early days, when all the science teaching was in the hands of one science teacher, I often slipped quietly into the laboratory for the mere joy of watching teacher and taught. The former seemed to live, move, and have her being there, for in and out, at all times, came girls bringing specimens, illustrations, curiosities, trying experiments on their own, and doing little jobs in preparation for the eagerly-anticipated lesson. There was a silence of a kind—not complete and not enforced, rather that silence which bespeaks an interest too deep for casual talk. The faces wore that purposeful expression which lends piquancy to the charm of youth. The mistress, small, pale, with quietly observant eyes and clear low voice, moved quickly from one to the other, correcting, explaining, here a word, there a deft touch, keeping the whole room intent and interested. With her heavy coronet of dusky hair and pretty blue overall she too made a picturesque figure. There are many intelligent young women in the world who owe their interest in science to her clever teaching and selfless service from which the school benefited for sixteen years. If she should ever read these words, she will know that her quondam headmistress not only rejoiced over such happy and successful work but also took a keen æsthetic delight in watching her classes at work. At their best—that is, at their most natural—schoolgirls are sweet, and childhood grace a very real thing.

I found it hard to decide what science was best for my school. The aim of science teaching is twofold: to train the mind and impart information. In a satisfactory syllabus, the latter should satisfy the native curiosity of the normal child and is therefore not all of one kind. The science we needed at Snellham was general, not highly specialized. Of this I was fully aware, but how to arrange for what might be described as a general smattering, avoid the appearance of superficiality, and satisfy examiners?

Two American girls applying for admission to the school told me they had ' done ' Chemistry, Physics, Biology, Astronomy, and Geology. When I expressed surprise, they explained that they only wanted to ' be able to talk about them '. No Britisher would own to such a motive, but to spend much time on Chemistry and remain in complete ignorance of Biology, or to learn Botany and be at a loss when a knowledge of Physics is needed, is almost as bad. If I had been clear of the examination bogey, I should have arranged for a five-year course of four weekly periods, the first four years to be spent on a general elementary course—Chemistry, Physics, Biology—and the fifth in more specialized work, each girl being free to choose her special subject from those included in the general course. Other schools, other syllabuses. Such a course would have been usefully illuminating to the Snellham type of girl.

Although there were practical difficulties in the way of teaching it, Botany was the most popular of the sciences that figured from time to time on the school timetable, and Chemistry the most unpopular. Botanical rambles belied their name unless we were able to set aside time enough to escape as far as the black-green countryside. Bulbs filled an empty space in our affections and, as we had a big dark cupboard available, tulips, daffodils, crocuses, and little blue scillas brightened our hall and form rooms when, at long last, spring replaced our long gloomy winter. Also, by much digging and dinner-hour labour, the girls, working in gangs, delighted in culti-vating the garden in front of the school so that flowering currant, wallflowers, and irises—sooty but very welcome—presented a cheery appearance at the school entrance. Once or twice during war-time, we divided the school into gangs and topdressed our playing field at the rear of the main building. The girls enjoyed working in gangs and even the staff joined in the happy enterprise. I approached the governors about the provision of a small greenhouse in a certain window embrasure. I was hard put to it to get the right specimens in abundance for the examination forms, and hoped to eke these out by home growths. My suggestion was opposed by a governor who lived in the vicinity of the town, who said that he was a botanist and had always found abundance of specimens, and that we had not gone far enough in our search. I asked my botany mistress what orders were represented in the flora of the neighbourhood and, armed with this information, renewed my request. When the botanist heard of *orders* he asked what they were and, in the end, I achieved—a cucumber frame. Round this we cultivated a small kitchen garden—Snellham was not fond of vegetables and I had an idea of rousing interest in this highly vitaminous range of food-stuffs. The first-year girls were the gardeners, and the lessons were given in the Botany periods. They worked in gangs and their labours were rewarded. Our usual crops were peas, beans, cabbages, and lettuces, but one season we grew specimens of every vegetable grown in England. I was sometimes presented with first-fruits, and, as I cut the lettuces into salad, I regarded their toughness as due to struggles against adverse conditions and, when I was trying to masticate them, I felt that in very truth they were of the substance from which the heroic is made, and regretted that I had not a more appreciative palate and a more adequate digestion to offer them. Later when, as I have already indicated, a change in the local industries made botanizing somewhat more productive, I used to rejoice to meet little biologists afield on Saturdays and holidays, optimistically carrying tins of various shapes and poking into bushes and ponds. Science teaching should lead to hobby-forming. I always appreciate that petition in Kipling's empire day hymn:

> Teach us delight in simple things.

Delight in simple things is a great safeguard in life.

English was the last subject to have a specialist, and the first one stayed long enough to be the senior of three or four. She was one of my ' crowning mercies '—I had several. When I had her ' adoption tried ' I followed old Polonius's advice and grappled her to my soul ' with hoops of steel '. She was a radiant teacher, and what that means to a school only those in the school can appreciate. She was gifted in an unusual way: she could speak the truth in love and at the same time effectively and she could be angry—very angry—and sin not. Her popularity proved that, given the right sort of reputation, tact is unnecessary. Naturally sharp-tempered, she struck out sharply when she felt strongly, but no one was hurt by her sharp speeches because her selflessness was apparent to all. Miss English—for so I shall call her— had a talent for scolding. Personally I have no use for

scolding and disapprove of it. But her scoldings seemed
to have no evil results. I remember once I was in the
room in which she was correcting exercises. Suddenly
she flushed with anger at some bit of bad work, jumped
up exclaiming, " I'll tell her what I think of her," and
left the room to do so. I could not avoid a little anxiety
as to what she would do, but she came back in a few
minutes remarking, as she resumed her work, and with
an unctuous self-satisfaction such as Macbeth would
have given the eyes out of his head to feel, " I've flayed
her alive." Her bloodthirsty operations never left an
unpleasant trail, and I was reassured when I caught sight
of her and her resuscitated victim in the corridor, discussing the faulty exercise. Said an anxious mother when
she left, " I could kiss her feet in my gratitude. Ethel
would have failed in English if she hadn't taken her at
odd times for extra work." Great is the force of selflessness: it covers a multitude of failings.

Miss English possessed that power of imperceptible
control which I valued so highly and in her subject there
was ample scope for its exercise. She did not relax her
grip on either class or individual, but organized so as to
allow freedom and opportunity for self-expression. In
this context, I recall the fourth form lecture club, which
held its meetings two or three times a term in the English
timetable periods, the members of which were each required to read two papers per session on subjects of their
choice. On the occasions on which I was present, Miss
English and I sat apart, the chair at the mistress's desk
being occupied by the president. As each of the three

or four lecturers finished her paper, the president invited criticism as to *matter*, *style*, *delivery*, assessing marks by show of hands. The girls managed the whole business promptly and effectively. A by-law allowed girls who were unable to hear the lecturer to open books and read as a protest against indistinct enunciation, but in a very short time the law was found to be unnecessary. The subjects were, I thought, somewhat commonplace: I remember being enlightened on Pigeons, and interested in A Holiday in Ireland (snapshots were handed round), Queen Victoria's Girlhood, and Reformers. The last began with the statement, " As it is easier to make men free than to make them good I shall begin with the religious reformer."

As far as one can judge of another, I believe Miss English was intellectually honest. English mistresses are exposed to special temptations to be otherwise. There are so many fantastic methods of teaching which lead to no result but which sound large and modern. I believe it was she who, during a discussion at a teachers' conference about the cultivation of initiative and self-expression, suddenly asked, " What if the little dears have nothing to express?" No one ever set a greater value on these qualities, as all her work showed, but she felt that it was still more important to provide something to express. " Ideas," she used to say, " work themselves out more easily than they work themselves in." The gaining of fresh ideas became a hobby with many of her pupils. I have heard of its leading girls to church or chapel— preference being given to the one that provided the more *ideas*—and I once felt bound to investigate the truth of a rumour that note books had been smuggled into back pews, on occasions when sermons on topical subjects or new books had been advertised. On Monday morning she set aside a few minutes with her form during which the girls were bound in honour to give the form the benefit of any new experiences they had had during the week-end. Thus a community of ideas was formed: newspaper cuttings, photographs, descriptive letters from overseas, summaries of books read, even new words and phrases were pooled for the general advantage. My heart warms and I laugh as I recall these eager collectors of *ideas*—it was good for their souls as well as their minds.

The Literary and Debating Society, which included the girls of the fifths and sixths—about ninety girls in all—was organized in the same self-governing way. When early in the session these girls had elected the committee, Miss English left them to ballot for the officials—president and secretary. She herself was a referee, her chief contribution being suggestions as to subjects. This committee was extremely autocratic. The girls were told what they had to do or read—the fiat went forth and was obeyed. After this length of time, I do not feel sure that even conviction was allowed its full weight. The debates were always spirited and sometimes more. I often marvelled at the total lack of fuss and palaver in the opening formalities. Snellham girls should make useful committee women. I did not often attend debates but always the literary evenings. The meetings were on Friday and preceded by a picnicky sort of tea managed by the girls

alone. I remember one evening devoted to the poetry of
Mr. Yeats. The girls were sitting in semicircles at one
end of the large hall, the lights of which had not been
switched on at the other, so that, when I slipped in behind,
I sat in semi-darkness. I saw their grave faces as they
recited *The Stolen Child* and other poems, sang *The Lake
Island of Innisfree* and *The Cloths of Heaven*, and took
parts in reading aloud *The Land of Heart's Desire*, and
listened to young voices reading of a land

> Where even the old are fair
> And even the wise are merry of tongue.

The delicate and mystical beauty of the poetry wrought
in me and its effect persisted into the restful seclusion of
my week-end. I believe both mystery and mysticism are
inherently attractive to our twi-lit minds and that our
holy religion gains as much as its loses by its mysteries.
I should never go so far as to say *credo quia impossibile*,
but I understand something of the mind of the man who
said it.

The Snellham girls had a poor literary endowment,
but a surprisingly keen literary appreciation which I
tried to analyse. It astonished me that girls who wrote
English faultily should show good taste in literature. I
once asked a rosy-cheeked fourth form girl, who was
learning a Browning poem on her own, why she liked
Browning. Her reply was not very illuminating: " He
seems to mean what he says and has good thoughts."
I interpret the first part of her answer to refer to the
force of his style: otherwise I am at a loss with regard

to the child's meaning.   The girls of the same form once appealed against my decision to let them act some modern play instead of their usual scenes from Shakespeare.   An inspectress who came straight to my room from a lesson of the Literary Sixth told me that the girls barely looked up when she went into their room, so engrossed were they in what they were reading.   My feelings were mixed when on inquiry I found the subject of such engrossing interest was De Quincey's *Murder as one of the fine arts!*

As our hall was furnished with a small stage, footlights, and a drop-curtain, it was easy for us to specialize in dramatic work.   Nothing had so great an effect on the personality of the girls, especially in developing initiative and affording scope for self-expression.   For many years I was able to arrange that every girl should have two, if not three, chances of showing what she could do on the stage: first during her first or second year, in her fourth, and often in her sixth.   All girls love acting, and in accordance with my principle of leaving no one out, every girl had a rôle, some, of course, more important than others.   It was a matter of surprise to me that we encountered little jealousy on that score: a happy state of things which was due, I believe, to the whole-hearted enjoyment of rehearsals, the fun of rummaging in property boxes and adapting costumes.   It was a big business to find plays to fit some ninety first-year girls and, as I write, I glow with gratitude to those members who gave voluntary help in the great enterprise.   The game was worth the candle.   It was a chief joy to the little eleven-year-olds, and the training they received in speech, deportment, and in scores of other ways was soon evident and lasted throughout their school life, probably longer. Dramatics and dancing enlivened the winter terms as games the summer. We made little of staging, and, although parents were invited to see the finished performances, there was nothing of the school show about them. When we gave entertainments for our school charities or to buy books or pictures for the school, the cast was mainly sixth form and chosen to suit the exigencies of the play. The happiest result of form dramatics is general chumminess.

I was hard put to it to devise a method of attacking the heavy provincial accent of young Snellham. The dramatics did much but not enough. Frequent correction of little faults is easily mistaken for nagging. It is futile to expect children to think about their little faults of speech or deportment—to hold up their heads or sound their aitches. Children can *think*, but they cannot do what a guardian of my youth—who hailed from Yorkshire—was always telling me to do—'think on'. Nor is it advisable that they should 'think on', growing self-conscious in the process. So I tried to devise some means of avoiding the necessity, and at length evolved something as follows. I chose a sentence made up largely of words commonly mispronounced, announced it weekly at the assembly, and the girls practised it. I believe the first I hit upon was the slogan, " Play up and play the game." (Our besetting sins were broad, flat A's, and a confusion between the various sounds of the vowel U.) I once began to compose a story—the staff ironically dubbed it the ' saga '—and doled it out sentence by sentence for practice. The younger children were always excited when the next instalment was due, and I used to hear them practising it during those last few minutes just before the bell rings to begin afternoon school. The first sentence ran: "Uncle Duncan and Aunt Grace lived in a lovely bungalow on Lake Ullswater, in Cumberland;" names and other details about their family followed, ending up with a baby named Blanche. It was a simple device but marvellously effective. Taken with the dramatic training, the accent of my sixth came to be free from taint of provincialism and the older forms soon outgrew the need for practising the ' saga '.

The dead hand of examination pressure hindered much good work in English as in other subjects. Our great difficulty was to inspire the girls with such a love of what is fine in literature that they read for reading's sake, not because the English mistress required them to do so. This difficulty may be encountered in all schools, but it is more acute in such schools as mine, and I do not think we ever solved it to a satisfactory extent. At one time, I believe that a certain examination paper actually played some part in solving the problem. I allude to a general literature paper set, many years ago, in one or other of the local examinations, which had for its object the testing of the general reading of the candidates. I allowed my girls the option of preparing themselves for it and they took to the idea, formed reading groups, met at one another's homes, and read more widely than before or since. A wide choice of question introduced a sporting element into the preparation, and I was aware of repressed excitement when the examiner was distributing the papers. The compulsory question was a list of quotations, easily recognizable by anyone who had read the poem, essay, or book from which it was taken, but not by anyone else—about twenty in all, full marks being given for, say, ten correct answers. This would be followed by a question requiring a short account of, say, three of the following: Meg Merrilies, Sir Patrick Spens, Diana of the Crossways, Sohrab and Rustum, Mrs. Malaprop, Autolycus, Mrs. Poyser and so on; and a third would give scope for wider knowledge by asking for an account of the use of the supernatural in Shakespeare, *or* of Elizabethan lyrics, *or* of one of the nineteenth-century essayists. I recognize that such a paper might encourage superficiality in reading, but discursive reading is better than none. Appetite comes sometimes while eating: perhaps it may come while nibbling. I know that, for the time being, several of my girls read good literature more widely than before, but I have no proof that it ever led to the formation of a habit of such reading.

Apropos of the cultivation of the initiative and the desirability of self-expression, both important objectives in education, I had an experience which showed me how easily the best ideals may lead themselves to perversion. A young mistress, nearing the end of her probationary year, had never taught in my presence because, whenever I visited her classes, I found the girls doing work on their own. One day, I found her giving directions to a first form to ' write a dialogue between any two people you like on any subject you like '. I returned at the end of the

appointed time to hear what had been written. The
mistress chose one representative from each of the six
rows of desks—there was not time to hear more. Nora
was chosen to begin. " My dialogue is between a lady
who wants her house decorated and the man who is going
to decorate it." " Proceed," said the mistress. Nora
proceeded, but was stopped. " You are swallowing your
words; begin again." Nora, who was at that stage of
growth when the tongue seems too large for the mouth,
tried to speak more distinctly and failed. To ease the
situation, I ventured a little compliment. " You seem to
know a great deal about house decoration, Nora." " We
are decorators," said Nora, in the tone of one whose
social position is assured. She recovered her spirits, and
the dialogue dragged its slow length along until the bell
rang and a postponement of the other five dialogues was
arranged. I pointed out to the mistress that the reading
of their own aimless piffle did the girls little good. She
replied, almost ecstatically: " Oh, Miss Cleeve, think of
the initiative." I did think about that and about much
else. She was an honours graduate of one of the older
universities and her teaching diploma was endorsed ' very
good '.

For classes who have no Latin, I found it helpful
towards the formation of a habit of selecting words and
phrases and the cultivation of a fine discrimination to
give two or three lessons in oral composition. To write
on the board the opening sentences of an essay and ask
the class to continue it, is one way of getting them to
realize the niceties of language. Discussions will follow

as to whether *a taste for* or *an inclination towards* best suits the context, whether *encouragement* or *inspiration* is the apt word and whether a participial phrase or an adverbial sentence forms the correct balance. Girls who have once or twice heard the teacher of such a lesson reject the flamboyant in favour of the precise will remember that words must not be used haphazardly, and that there is always the apt word if trouble is taken to find it. The short stories in the Bible are well-known examples of simple effectiveness and I have found them delightfully useful models.

The acquisition of knowledge needs effort, and effort is good for everyone and absolutely essential to human progress. I was down on slacking wherever I found it. Steady, happy work injures no one, but worry kills. Examinations may be enjoyable: I have known them to be so. When my school was small and the teaching did not make such heavy demands on the staff, for seven happy years we never knew what failure in examinations meant and the girls never worried. Later, they did. I repeat that the only way of lessening the ordeal of preparation for examinations is to keep a high standard of work in the lower forms so that the girls may feel that they have a good chance of passing, in which case worry is reduced to a minimum. When girls know that their future careers may be affected adversely by a poor leaving certificate, no power avails to keep them carefree. It is a realization of these facts that floods my soul with gratitude when I call to mind the devoted labours of both Miss English, who was a most successful examination teacher, and her colleague, Miss Maths, our senior mathematical specialist, at first the only one, later the head of a department with four subordinates. As a result of work her Snellham girls did not often worry seriously about their chance of success in that subject: they thought they were going to pass and, from the point of worry, that is as good as passing. Miss Maths inspired trust: she was a radiant teacher, and richly endowed by nature, physically and mentally. Trustworthiness was appreciated in Snellham, where the world was too much for most of us, and where everyone seemed to be looking for a helper. " When Mary gets into Miss Maths' classes, she'll be all right—Miss Maths won't let her waste her time "—those words or the substance of them were uttered scores of times by anxious mothers whose daughters were getting out of their control, and who looked, as so many did, to the school discipline to supplement their own. Miss Maths believed in the life strenuous: her classes were the busiest and the happiest in the school. I have referred to the *knack* of teaching. In her case, it almost amounted to conjuring. Said one of her pupils to a newcomer, who in my presence had explained that she was ' bad at mathematics ': " It's no good saying you can't do riders. Before you know where you are, you'll be getting one out." Miss Maths reared her little mathe- maticians on problems from the days of the multiplica- tion tables, and was cute enough to rope into the school exercises their youthful zest for puzzles. Very few girls were unable to take mathematics in their examinations, and I often found it difficult to induce girls who were slow and delicate to drop the subject. I attribute many of the characteristics of the school to the thoroughness of the mathematical training—the general directness of outlook, the almost entire absence of affectation, the impatience at fuss and palaver and disdain of ' sloppiness ', and feel sure it accentuated what was native in young Snellham—persistency in the face of failure. Mathematical training leaves a more permanent effect on the mentality than any other except perhaps that very rare thing—a thorough grounding in the classics.

Miss Maths was an interesting disciplinarian. First of all she kept her classes busy. Secondly, she never got into muddles, clearheadedness being one of her many gifts. Thirdly, she had the advantage of having been a naughty schoolgirl herself, and fellow-feeling made her wondrous kind and very keen. No one could evade her calm scrutiny. As a delinquent once described her to me, she had ' open eyes ' (I interpreted this as referring to her steadfast, clear gaze, straight into one's eyes). Her classes were very rowdy, if one judged from the sounds—of arguments, derision, dispute, and amusement—which issued from them. " I've left them to quarrel it out," she explained when I came upon her, compasses in hand and covered with chalk, standing outside the form room. " They do enjoy catching me out in a mistake," she said proudly, when she had owned to being hot and heckled after a very ' interesting ' class. When I went into her classes I always felt guilty of wanton disturbance as they seemed always ' just on the point of getting it out ', and if I called her away for a moment, the head girl would slip into her place, finish the problem and begin the next. Her ' home work ' exercises needed little supervision, although they were one and a half hours long. This I attributed to the fact that she promptly corrected them and had a quick, thorough method of bringing home to the class, individually and collectively, the mistakes made. On such apparent trifles does effectiveness often depend. " Strike while the iron is hot " is a good motto for the corrector of exercises who desires that her classes should learn from their mistakes. Taken as a whole, I should describe her perfect and unique discipline as a triumph of personality; she neither punished, reported, nor scolded, but *insisted*—pleasantly and with an air of finality. The first inspector who visited her classes warned me that she had ' a spice of the devil in her eye '. I did not feel alarmed, as I am fond of condiments, liking a good deal of pepper in my soup. Throughout our long colleagueship I found her delightfully stimulating, and the success of our mathematical side was evidence of the excellence of her work. In a subtle but very real way, the school outlook became mathematical. Miss Maths had an eye for humorous situations, and mirth and maths came to be linked together in a way I never quite understood: even a passing allusion to the subject in assembly would elicit gurgles. (I like schoolgirl gurgles as much as I dislike schoolgirl giggles.) I remember once setting a Scripture question to a third form, the first half of which required a life of Saul the king. To my surprised amusement, a girl supplemented her answer with what she meant to be a graph.

The curve went up and down, the beginning being labelled as equal to ' *seeking the asses* '; the highest as equal to *Zenith, God save the king*; the lowest of all as equal to *miserable death on Mount Gilboa*. The writer's grade of intelligence may be guessed from the answer to the second part of the question—about the lessons to be learnt from Saul's failures. " We may learn," she wrote, " from his failures when we have reached our zenith to stick to it with a right good will."

I believe I valued Miss Maths more as a sixth form mistress than as a specialist; she was so exactly what I desired my sixth to be—purposeful, sincere, sporting, reliable—and I delegated my work with the sixth to her without a misgiving. Many of her pupils emulated her in so far as training as mathematical specialists at various universities and are now doing such work. How much I hope they are also reproducing her loving kindness and strength of purpose! For she had yet higher qualities than I have mentioned. Quick in detecting slackness, she had a still quicker eye for those who needed help and sympathy. She never missed a little down-and-out: an unhappy child, naughty or good, was sure of her notice. As I review such of her dealings as came to my knowledge, I find myself repeating a doggerel verse of my childhood days:

> Who ran to kiss me when I fell
> And did some pretty story tell,
> And kissed the place to make it well?

The connexion is a subtle one, because in the whole

course of our close fellowship I never heard of her using a word of endearment, and only once do I remember her kissing anyone (unless someone first kissed her and, even then, I have my doubts). She detested caresses of all kinds. The distinction between her and that other radiant teacher was that Miss English regarded the girls as those whom she was helping towards a full and successful life and preparing for a career. To Miss Maths the girls were young wayfarers on the highroad of life who needed help and sympathy and comfort as well as equipment. When she was about to leave, I witnessed some shedding of painful tears and heard many expressions of sorrow, and the whining of the lame dogs whom she was helping over stiles, sounded long and piteously in my ears.

I once was taken seriously to task by an inspector for alluding to Art as a ' recreative subject '. It all arose from my habit of putting art teaching in the upper forms in the afternoon, when even young people cannot possibly feel as fresh as in the morning. I still regard it as a relief after the heat of the scholastic day is over and when some parts of us may safely relax. I rejoice that art in schools is a very different thing from the travesty of it which I suffered under, when we were given freehand copies to reproduce and taught nothing about the general principles underlying the subject. Nowadays the aim of art teaching is to provide by means of craftsmanship an outlet for the creative instinct, and the teaching of artistic appreciation is a most important part of the training.

The force of suggestion plays a great part in getting good work from an art class. I am much impressed by what I saw of its efficacy. It underlies the artist-in-every-child theory. Some of my staff had the knack of using it more than others: the girls were given the work to do and did it, there being no suggestion of inability. The results were varied and delightful to remember. I do not refer to those painful studies of still life and sickly water-colours which we used to perpetrate and give to our parents and friends, but to the designing and decorating of beautiful things for use and also adornment. But there is a deeper side to art training than craftsmanship. To appreciate may be possible for those who fail in execution. Carlyle says somewhere that it is a tragedy for a man to die ignorant who has the capacity for knowledge. It is a tragedy for a man to live ignorant of beauty in a world so beautiful as ours. I have known art mistresses so keen on craftsmanship that they forgot to open the eyes of their pupils to the beauty of the world in general. Indeed, I have sometimes wondered whether they themselves were alive to it. It is a tragedy that it is impossible for so many of us to visit the great galleries where the world's masterpieces are to be found. " Give us bread and give us roses," says a little poem, probably written by some member of the Independent Labour Party. It is true that man cannot live—in the sense that God intended him to live—without beauty, for which there is a deep-seated longing in many young souls.

We have to be thankful for the picture galleries within our reach and for the effort made to reproduce in colour some of the finest of the world's pictures. The latter have an effect on the taste of children. I remember being delighted when a fourth form complained bitterly that, during the holidays, their reproduction of Raphael's *Madonna del Granduca* had been replaced by a Greuze, and expressed their feelings by describing the latter as ' more like the picture on a chocolate box '. Hard on Greuze, I admit, but the preference was in the right direction. When the teaching of artistic appreciation is in the hands of those who, themselves, are to be classed among *les beaux esprits qui s'entendent*, then will the love of cheap effects, of over elaboration and crude colouring, in a word, the formation of unworthy ideals, cease.

We worked hard to get good pictures for the school, and were encouraged by gifts from the wife of our first chairman and from casual visitors to the school. By sixth-form entertainments we amassed money to provide the new hall with Medici prints, the first of which had just been published. After an expenditure of about forty pounds and a special journey of prefects and self to the nearest agency, I felt the occasion merited some notice from the governing body, and after alluding in my report to the purchase, I had the pictures arranged in the committee room for them to see. No, not a word. I have no evidence that any of them so much as looked at the little show at the end of the room. The town hall keeper who helped me to arrange was much impressed, and the chief constable, whom I met on the steps of the town hall, said, " A mighty fine show those pictures of yours. Are you going to make any more such gifts to the town?" Some days later one of the governors remarked that he thought the portraits of the governors would look well in the hall. I was scared stiff, and never again, either in committee or out, alluded to our need for pictures.

If there should turn out to be a reincarnation, I shall ask to be endowed with a more commanding presence in whatever shape I may have to assume. I feel I was a prey to inspectors with a turn for lecturing. One such was much exercised lest I should be led astray in the direction of over-emphasis on the domestic arts. He had probably heard some unfavourable reports of our needlework and was afraid that I should yield to pressure and devote too much time to it. " Your committee will probably regard your school as a continuation of the elementary education of the town, and badger you about producing elaborate needlework. Take no notice. Your business is to teach the girls to think." I understand what he meant. In such a town as Snellham then was, unused to higher education, the tendency is to stress the three R's and needlework. We taught the latter only for the first two years; after which followed four terms of cookery and two of laundry work. The examination forms did no domestic work of any kind, and in the sixth, only those girls who were studying to become elementary school teachers. It is a mistake to confuse the two types of education; one of which is planned to stop at fourteen or thereabouts and the other to continue at least two years longer. They are essentially different.

Physical culture is of prime importance in a hard-working, examination-ridden school, and when I was sketching out the timetable for the session, I invariably filled in the organized-games periods first of all and, on principle, I allowed nothing to interfere with those periods. To make girls interested in games, there must be fixtures. My ideal was to have one period *per diem* in every form given to physical exercise—either drill or games. I was not able to arrange for this in the middle school but usually at the top, and always at the bottom, of the school. The senior school had an afternoon for games to allow of teams being chosen from any of the senior forms. I felt the importance of removing every obstacle in the way of effective organization. Games, if they are to assist in development, must be played with zest and bring pleasure to the players. We got the best out of games when the principle of self-government was recognized. Especially is the spirit of happy freedom necessary in the playing of matches. If a girl expects to be called to account for poor play by any but her fellows, she will run in invisible shackles. Girls who are keen at sport—and only such will be elected to the committee if the girls are allowed a free hand—may be trusted to choose players even for important school matches. A games mistress who is good at her job will get her own way in most respects because a suggestion from her will be as potent as a command, but she must first win the trust of the committee and avoid mistakes in judgment. Far better to risk defeat than go counter to the opinion of the games committee and lose the match after all. Health and happiness should be the outcome of games, even organized games. And what lessons of subordination of self to the common good, of restraint in victory, of dignity in defeat, in short of " affirming one's own personality while allowing others a chance of affirming theirs "—are to be learnt on a school playing-field!

Drill is another thing altogether, but well taught it should produce both pleasure and profit. With some teachers, tasks seem light, with others, even pleasures are unpleasant. I am convinced that a school is disgraced by a slouching heavy-footed girl in the same way as it is when a girl spells badly. Occasionally it is impossible to cure either a bad carriage of the head or defective ortho- graphy. But usually a girl's deportment depends as much on how she is drilled as on how she is made. A drill mistress who knows how to make taut the flaccid muscle and who takes pains with individuals can work great marvels in changing clumsiness into grace and inducing correct balance and steady poise. I encouraged my girls to dance—at morning break, in the dinner hour, when outdoor games were not possible, even before school when a squally, unexpected shower had drenched the unprepared. As a whole the Snellham girls were graceful; in games agile rather than weighty. The one occasion when I swelled with a pride which could not be concealed was when the school team was playing a losing game in one of our district games league tournaments. I admire pluck and the Snellham girls had it. They never knew when they were beaten, and when I left there were already two shields on the walls of the hall which had been won after a long series of yearly contests in our district games league.

CHAPTER IX

My Experience of the Municipal Control of Education

Whenever headmistresses are to be found in conclave, the topic of local control of education is bound sooner or later to come up for discussion. The discussions I heard were many and monotonous, indeed a veritable harping on one note. I am not inclined to believe that Snellham was noticeably worse than the average. In municipal affairs much depends upon the town—its size and main preoccupations.

The Snellhamites had a low opinion of their municipal rulers. They elected them and then consistently crabbed them. It is the same in other towns of the same size. Even if we allow for the Englishman's habit of grumbling at his own, and for the tendency which would seem to be inherent in him of saying *nihil nisi malum*, this fact needs explanation. The cause may be found to some degree in the exaggerated effect of *esprit de corps* which prevails to advance the cause of the intriguer against the judgment of the wise, and may be the reason why so many of the latter stand aloof from municipal affairs. Indeed, when I review my experience of municipal government in

Snellham and call to mind what I have heard of other towns, I feel like that disagreeable child who, after reading the epitaphs in a churchyard, asked where the wicked people were buried. My inquiry would be about the good people still above ground—so rarely do they seem to find their way into the local borough councils.

The charge most often brought against municipal leaders is that they are prompted by self-interest, or, to use the common phrasing, have *axes to grind*. This is probably true of most of us. Only the very elect (we call them saints) have no axes to grind. Axes vary and so do the methods of grinding them. Some councillors bring very heavy axes and secure the first place at the grindstone, on the plea that ' business is business '. With others, the notoriety gained is an axe with two edges, one heavier than the other, as likewise is the patronage which induces servility in the needy, and delights the small souls who practise it. I ascribe much of general unpopularity to this cause. People will eat humble pie to secure preferential treatment for themselves or their families, but in their hearts they resent the necessity. " If you don't eat off their plate and drink out of their cup they'll get their knife into you," was the fiercely resentful utterance of one who had had a thrust from the knife. A fellow headmistress once said to me that the chief quality needed for success in municipal life was *a low cunning*. I should have said it was servility of soul or, as Snellham phrased it, willingness to *kow-tow*. Nothing in retrospect delights me more than the fact that I gained a reputation for independence. I may have suffered for it at the time, but in retrospect I rejoice over it.

I judge that the members of town councils wherever found conform to certain types. There are wire-pullers and their puppets to be found in most towns—men ready to do disagreeable work at the prompting of those whose pleasure it is to exert indirect rather than direct influence, and in whose power it lies to repay in favours more or less substantial. There is the conscientious objector who caves in to the prevailing *esprit de corps* after some little effort at independence. Latterly there has appeared the political extremist who finds capital in municipal affairs and the die-hard who resists him without suffering the pains of dissolution. The municipally-minded women are of the kind described as *estimable*. They support, ably and consistently, all proposals for the betterment of the race including education, and are usually found " on the right side " in other matters. They have earnest faces with noses well adapted for looking down and over. Their conception of duty is not so much the confirming of the Right as the righting of the Wrong. Hence their chief (official) pastime is mare's-nesting.

I began my official life with a genuine admiration for what is called a sense of duty; when I closed it, I had come to see that there is a much more excellent way of service and to distrust duty as a motive. Before the psychologists told us that there was no such thing as pure philanthropy, by self-examination I had come to disbelieve in the existence of unmixed motive in *unaided* man. A sense of duty so very easily, in *unaided* man or woman, becomes a disguise for personal rancour, and general self-seeking. Alas, poor human nature! " I thought it was the voice of God and it was the voice of the devil," said the miserable hero of a well-known novel as he slunk home in the darkness. There are few more pathetic utterances in fiction. Moreover, a sense of duty takes us only a very little way along the path of service. I should feel it grotesque to connect duty with St. Francis's inspired extravagances and irreverent to associate it with Our Lord. As I read the gospel story, Christ came, saw, pitied, loved, healed, helped, pouring out the riches of His wisdom, and the passion and power of God came upon Him so that He became the Saviour of the world by His Life as by His Death. Duty with its self-regarding limitations had nothing to do with His way of saving and, let us make no mistake, it has little to do with ours. At best I should say of Duty in this respect what Tennyson says of Knowledge when comparing her with Wisdom:

> Let her know her place;
> She is the second, not the first.

But, in spite of conforming to certain municipal types, I feel sure that Snellham developed peculiarities because its social make-up was peculiar. It was a town of one or two great industries. The directors of these industries and their families took an active share in the life of the town, and their underlings, the managers of departments, did likewise. This curtailed the freedom of the town while making a notable contribution to its well-being in many directions. Freedom, as the psychologist reaffirms —we knew it before—is essential to normal development. Snellham suffered from this curtailment. On the other hand, the Pigirons, as I will call them for convenience, were full of good works, and seemed to divide the religious and philanthropic work of the town between them. The subscription lists of all the town charities were sure of a good initiation by a list of Pigiron names; no good cause lacked patronage and support from one or other of the families; they lent grounds for fêtes and held drawing-room meetings for deserving causes; they read lessons in the churches and opened bazaars galore. The rest of the town followed suit, if somewhat listlessly. Their standard —a steady mediocrity plus excellence in business—was the subconsciously accepted one for the town.

Owing to this Pigiron pervasiveness there was not much scope for climbers and thrusters in municipal affairs, the chairmanships of the important committees falling naturally to the Pigirons. Those of secondary importance were eagerly sought after and, when gained, regarded as a means to one end, viz. self-display in municipal activity. We have all learnt to regard self-assertion with an indulgent eye. So much good has modern psychology effected that we find it easier to obey the apostolic injunction, " Consider thyself lest thou also be tempted." But the rivalry between the various committees was marked: the gas was jealously aware of the doings of the electricity; if the borough treasurer got a ' rise ', the chairman of the Health Committee asked for one for his chief official. The boys' school was pitted against the girls', and I once heard a cheery little Alderman at a prize-giving declare, with every sign of magnanimity, " *Although* I am the chairman of the elementary education committee, *yet* I am a friend to secondary education." (The italics are both his and mine.)

For a score of years I enjoyed peace (comparatively speaking) under chairmen of the Pigiron kind, but later my turn came to suffer under one of the second kind who, when he was securely seated, looked round for something to do to distinguish his period of office. He suffered from a veritable *cacoethes agendi*, which I was at no pains to allay. He proposed building additions to our laboratory accommodation and invited me to apply for additional staff—both suggestions I was unable to accept, there being no immediate necessity for either. Worse than that, I had no serious difficulties to discuss with him, having been trained by my late chairman to settle things which concerned internal administration and which, strictly speaking, could not be settled by anyone else without violating the instrument of school government. This was a blunder which cost me dearly. To ask advice is to flatter. I was either too stupid or too honest to avail myself of this means of ingratiating myself.

There is another reason for consulting governors to which I shrink from referring, and shall do so only in-directly by narrating two well-worn anecdotes in the expectation that their juxtaposition and common element will convey my meaning to those familiar with the methods of intelligence tests. (i) A missionary who had worked in some remote part of the world told his audiences that the thing that troubled him most was that the natives could not understand anyone liking to be alone and suspected such of sinister designs. He hardly dared to pray in secret lest his influence for good should suffer. (ii) A mother busy at the washtub said to her daughter, "Mary, go and see what Tommy is doing and tell him he mustn't." Let him that readeth understand.

I began my official life with a genuine regard for my governors, who were as kind to me as they knew how to be, but I found the meetings very depressing and often had an attack of the blues after one. I was young and not yet self-contained. I longed for some acknowledgment of the success of the school and should have liked to know that I was ' giving satisfaction ', as the servants say. But it was never customary in Snellham to praise municipal officials, for two reasons: firstly, the members of the committee were too busy admiring themselves to be aware of anybody else's virtues; secondly, praise in the municipal mind was indissolubly connected with an increase in salary and Snellham was chronically hard up. During the quarter of a century of my headship I received only one sentence of commendation from any governor, male or female, in public or in private. When panegyrics appeared in the local press they made no reference to the headmistress and were appropriated by the chairman.

As time went on, I became accustomed to the idiosyncrasies of my governors and, after committee meetings, used to stave off depression and solace my soul with— not a verse from Holy Writ or a quotation from Browning, but the compressed wit and wisdom of our—yours as

well as mine—rude forefathers, as set forth in the proverb, " You can't expect anything from a pig but a grunt ".
I did not mean to be disrespectful to my governors (or
to pigs). This odd twist of thought and expression brought
comfort to my timid soul by intimating that the blame
for the lack of graciousness on the part of the governors
did not lie with *me*, that, indeed, there was no blame
at all. The governors were simply acting *convenienter
naturae*. Moreover, I like pigs, and consider them already
underrated. Not by the flicker of an eyelash, much less
by a proverb, would I hurt the feelings of a pig. I detect
a certain interrogative wistfulness in the tilt of his snout
as he gazes at me, unblinkingly it seems—owing to the
inadequacy of his eyelashes. He has qualities I admire.
There is, for instance, nothing sly or sinuous about him:
he is naked and unashamed as were (possibly) our ancestors before the adaptation of the fig leaf. I pity him:
it must be very hard to have to depend on one's nostrils,
however well developed, for self-expression. He has not
had his due. Someone ought to write a poem to the pig
as Mr. Chesterton has done so exquisitely for ' brother
ass '. So far only Charles Lamb has written in praise
of him, and it would be unreasonable to expect any pig
to be content with such a *post mortem* tribute as his
Dissertation. Perhaps some fine day (probably about
9 a.m.) the inward urge towards poetical expression in
favour of the pig may come to one of that not incon-
siderable class which Horace describes as *Epicuri de
grege porci*, in which case fellow feeling may strengthen
the urge and the pig be duly honoured.

The alchemy of Time work wonders. Not only does it change base metals into gold and (alas!) gold into baser metals, but (I am coming to this surprising conclusion) it is capable of turning past tragedy into present comedy. The process is gradual. What I thought was tragedy has toned down already to something like what the mechanicals of Athens described as ' most lamentable comedy '. I am concerned to know how far the process will go. Surely tragedy will never turn into farce?

In retrospect I see that I took things much too seriously and suffered accordingly. To headmistresses prone to the same weakness and still in the tragic vein I would say: " Bide a wee. You may yet die a-laughing." Blessed is the headmistress who can regard the follies and swagger of municipal humanity with tolerance and a twinkle in her eye. A twinkle in the eye must be a great asset to a headmistress. I was not fortunate in that respect, having no eyes worth speaking of behind my glasses. But in spite of shortsightedness, I thank God I could always lift them to the far distant hills from which came help. (Twinkling does no end of good: the heavens themselves would not seem nearly so sociable if the stars did not twinkle.)

I took my committees very seriously and always went well prepared—or should I say well armed? Yet they were often quite enjoyably funny. I retain a clear recollection of one which met about the time of the Board of Education's reorganization of secondary school examinations Hitherto we had entered pupils for the Oxford Local, and the first discussion was whether we should continue to do so. (As a matter of fact, the change to the new School Certificate of the neighbouring universities was inevitable, as the pupils in both girls' and boys' schools looked to these universities for scholarship assistance.) When I overheard one governor say to his neighbour, " We've had enough of Oxford "—the allusion being to a recent official in the committee's service, an Oxford man, who had left after treating them to a piece of his mind—I knew Oxford was down and out. Next came the question of substitute. The chairman of the technical education committee suggested an examination of which I had never heard the name, and which was reminiscent of county asylums as it included the word *institutes* and the names of two or more adjacent counties. But the suggestion received little support, as at that moment one of the women governors in a low, ladylike voice remarked that she had " heard that the College of Preceptors was a very nice (sic) examination ". The women governors rarely spoke in full committee—they displayed considerable activity in less overt ways—and when the unexpected happens, everyone listens. I forebore to interrupt, feeling sure that the suggestion was beloved of the author of its being and that the little darling must not be strangled at birth. So I dandled it a little before smothering it by reference to remorseless facts. It took a great deal of breath to demolish the College of Preceptors.

" He that knows not that he knows not is a fool," says the adage. As regards municipal control of education, there was never a truer word spoken. Several of the dozen men who sat gravely round that committee table were experts at their particular jobs, but they were fools that afternoon and many a time before and since. On municipal officials is laid the nauseating necessity of suffering fools not gladly—that's impossible—but tactfully. These things ought not so to be. The local education committee is responsible for the external organization of the education of county or borough, which includes the appointment of experts in the internal administration of its schools, that is of competent headmasters and headmistresses. The latter are responsible for the success of those schools as judged by inspectors and other experts and confirmed by public opinion. Some liaison arrangement is needed because the internal and external are interdependent, but in no case should the expert be obliged to listen to the advice of the inexpert. It is time to cut the cackle and get to business. Time is wasted as it was in the case I have quoted. The governors have a right to the fullest information as to what happens in the schools, and the heads have no right to withhold this or to refuse to give reasons, or answer questions—but that is all.

After all this, it pleases me to be able to say that for twenty-five years I lived on the best of terms with my governing body, being given all I asked for — I was careful to keep within bounds—and all the freedom which my instrument of government assigned to me. Indeed, I gained a reputation for getting my own way. I remember once the annual necessity for the renewal of two privileges led me to make my usual application, and to my surprise I met with a refusal. Puzzled and perturbed, I

rang up the chairman and kept at him until, on the point
of losing his temper, he rapped out: " You may have one
—I don't care which—but not both—*you must be chastised
somehow.*" I sought for the explanation of this cryptic
utterance, and, when I heard that someone had been
twitting him about ' letting Miss Cleeve have things all
her own way ', I understood the situation and quietly
took both. The idea of chastisement of officials was a
common one, and fault-finding regarded as a sacred duty
by those responsible for the educational welfare of Snellham, many of whom managed in this instance to make
their duty their delight.

The happiness of the head of a school depends largely
on his or her chairman, and, here again, I was fortunate
until within a few years of retirement. The first was the
best and the only one for whom I had the least personal
liking. He was not a fool, for he knew that he knew not
and insisted that I should have the freedom that was
mine by virtue of the instrument of school government.
" Leave the headmistress to manage the school," he would
rap out. " We're not a set of schoolmistresses." Those
were the last words I heard him say in committee, and
when I saw his funeral *cortège* pass, I knew that the first
fine careless rapture of my headmistress-ship—I speak
comparatively—was over and would never recur. Those
were halcyon days, and my heart leaps up in gratitude
when I realize what I owe to his reasonable view of things.

My second chairman was also of the opinion that he was
not a schoolmistress. He did not say so, but his non-
interference proved it. He also was not a fool: he knew

that he knew not. A genuine specimen of a downright man who was also upright, he preferred saying the disagreeable thing to one's face and could be trusted to defend the absent. I disliked him as much as he disliked me, but I had entire trust in his probity and he, being bored—as I always felt—with education in general and the school in particular, was relieved to leave the latter in my hands. This basis of mutual dislike and mutual trust proved quite workable. He rarely visited the school, and encouraged me to settle matters which were clearly within my province without reference to the committee, giving as his reason that he didn't see how anyone else could know anything about it. When a real crisis threatened, a sense of duty brought him up to the school. One such occasion occurred after I had given a lesson on French negatives and affirmatives, in which I had tried to incorporate some hints on English manners—a subject best treated impersonally and incidentally. In contrasting the politeness of ' Oui, Madame ' and ' Non, Monsieur ' with the abruptness of our ' Yes ' and ' No ', I had added some words such as the following: " We English people do not use the word *Sir* or *Madam*, but you may avoid the effect of abruptness by pronouncing the words *yes* and *no* gently and slowly." The chairman heard that I was telling the girls not to say *sir*. The pillars of civilization seemed to be tottering, and he rose to the urgency of the occasion. After a perfunctory greeting he began the interview by inquiring whether I thought there was too much reverence in the world. I replied that I did not. " Then why have you been at pains to tell your pupils not to use the word *sir?*" I explained my little attempt to teach manners, feeling sure he would approve of such a Victorian procedure. But he snapped out: " All very well, but *what* manners?" " Mine," I replied— just a shade too promptly. " I know no others." It was a pyrrhic victory, for he went away crosser than he came, and all headmistresses will agree that that is not the ideal ending to an interview with one's chairman. But to his credit on my retrospective balance sheet I must enter the fact that he was the only governor who ever commended me as having anything to do with the efficiency of the school. How clearly do I recall the exact occasion! There had been a Full Inspection (I cannot hold myself back from using capitals when writing those words); the governors were in session with the Inspectors (capitals again), and I was just resuming my seat after those minutes of absence when the discussion on the headmistress is supposed to take place. The chairman turned to me and congratulated me on the report just given. The shock was great and has imprinted itself on my memory. But I felt no elation. Thanks to my porcine proverb and the hardening effects of public life, I had grown indifferent to the opinion of anyone not immediately connected with the internal life of the school.

Snellham at that time paid little attention to the reports which were sent down after Full Inspection, and, indeed, at times seemed to consider the Board of Education itself as a superfluity. How could Whitehall judge of Snellham affairs as well as its town council? Moreover, it was suspected that such Inspectors as visited the secondary schools had a bias in favour of the schools, and in case of a conflict might even side with the headmaster or headmistress. Caution was needed. A polite hearing was usually vouchsafed, but advice was discounted and regulations ignored as long as possible. I was never so lacking in tact as to back up any of my own suggestions with a reference to the Board, as my one experience of the chill dignity which had followed such a solecism sufficed. Much water has flowed under bridges since my first chairman who—so I noticed—fidgeted considerably during the reading of such an inspection report, remarked to me at the end, " You managed them in a masterly way, Miss Cleeve," a remark with a barb in its tail. After the second Full Inspection, the second chairman followed me out of the room, remarking pleasantly, " You mustn't let all this make you too big for your boots." The coarseness of the mode of expression hurt me more than the remark itself.

Neither of these two chairmen enters vividly into the comedy of manners which my retrospective faculty is evolving. But the last chairman will do so. He differed from his predecessors in that he did not know that he did not know. It would seem, therefore, that he is cast for the rôle of Fool. But fools in plays are often so finely wise—think of the ' inspired babblings ' of Lear's poor Fool—and I could never class him alongside of, say, Touchstone. No. Should the comedy slither down further and become farce, then there will be a place for the little man.

Unlike his predecessor, he thought he was a schoolmistress, and it was on this account we differed. I held my own while trying to avoid hostilities. I even adopted the tactics of Mr. Lear's

> Old man who said, " How
> Shall I soften the heart of this terrible cow?
> I will sit on a stile and continue to smile
> Till I soften the heart of this cow."

No use at all. He wasn't that sort of cow: I don't suppose he even noticed anything more subtle than a guffaw, and I have never been able to accomplish much in the way of guffawing. Hostilities began. Had they been carried on according to the rules of the ring, I might have stood a chance of winning, for my opponent had about as much finesse as a cockchafer in a lighted room. Alas! he laid hold of a sledgehammer made of Pigiron's heaviest and best, and I staggered out of the arena murmuring in Mr. Henley's most inelegant, horribly hackneyed, but perfectly irresistible phrasing, " My head is bloody but unbowed."

And so to Innisfree.